Billfish
ON A
Fly

Billfish
ON A
Fly

BY JACK SAMSON

Frank Amato

PORTLAND

To Victoria

Photo Credits:
All photos by Jack Samson except
the following:
Neal Rogers: cover & back cover, 4-7
Linda Rogers: 1
Terri Gunn: 15
Jerry Jergens: 26, 39
Cam Sigler: 20, 28, 37B, 64-67, 76
Wes Ruggles: 43, 45
Chuck Rizuto: 62

Jack Samson

First Edition, 1995

Frank Amato Publications, Inc.
P.O. Box 82112 • Portland, Oregon 97282
503/653-8108

Printed in Hong Kong
Hardbound ISBN: 1-57188-018-6

(1 3 5 7 9 10 8 6 4 2)

Contents

FOREWORD

It is difficult for me to believe—in light of present-day enthusiasm for the sport of catching billfish on a fly—that 30 years ago almost nobody was doing it. There are few moments in the exciting fly fishing game that can compare with a lit-up billfish aggressively devouring a fly.

It all began with Dr. Webster Robinson and his wife, Helen, in the 50s and 60s. They developed the "tease and switch" technique that we all take for granted today. Dr. Robinson had passed away before I traveled to Ecuador in 1970 in search of a big striped marlin. But his widow was very generous with her counsel on tackle and technique before I departed for Salinas. I credit my success on that trip to her helpful advice.

And so there was a time in the early years when the very idea of catching these great fish on something as fragile as a fly rod and a delicate tippet was thought impossible. It can still be a formidable task since world record rules only allow 12 inches of heavy shock leader next to the fly. Then there must come at least 15 inches of the lightweight class tippet. A slashing bill can make short work of demolishing that tippet only a few inches from the fly, not to mention that a big marlin or sailfish can take that fly down to 15-20 inches in a big gulp and good-bye fly. However so many world records have been set with this regulation that the International Game Fish Association is reluctant to increase the allowed length of the shock tippet.

There have been vast improvements in rods, reels, lines, backing, leaders, flies and hooks, so that the scales have been tipped a little more in the direction of the angler. Many of the world's great fly anglers have lent their expertise to this tackle improvement, and to the innovations in technique that have improved hookup percentages.

Jack Samson is one of those anglers, and we have fished together in many parts of the world. I was delighted to hear that such an experienced angler, who also has a life-

Top: **Webster "Doc" Robinson, pioneer big game fly fisherman, watches as his wife, Helen, works a teaser rod.** *Middle:* **Billy Pate (left) the first fly rodder to catch Pacific black marlin, with his 16 pound tippet class world record 42 pound, 6 ounce black caught September 8, 1972 in Australia.** *Bottom right:* **"Doc" Robinson and his 145 pound Pacific striped marlin—the first caught on a fly— landed in 1965 off Baja California's East Cape.**

Left: **Billy Pate (right) and his world record 146 pound Pacific striped marlin—caught February 10, 1970 off Salinas, Ecuador on a 16 pound tippet.** *Middle:* **Pate's 16 pound tippet world record Atlantic sailfish of 75 pounds—caught September 18, 1975 off Venezuela.** *Right:* **The first Atlantic blue marlin ever caught on a fly—Pate's world record 96 pounder—landed August 21, 1978 on 16 pound tippet.**

time of writing and editorial experience, was undertaking the creation of this book.

Jack fished in the first billfish fly tournament that I put together in Islamorada, Florida in 1981. In 1989 the team of Jack Samson and Joe Hudson won the first annual International Billfish Fly Tournament in Costa Rica, which has been held there annually since then, the tournament being sponsored by World Wide Sportsman of Islamorada.

By 1974 I had taken Atlantic and Pacific sailfish, black, white and striped marlin on a fly rod. My burning ambition was always to catch a blue marlin on a fly, which no one had ever done before. They are the toughest fish in the sea. After making attempts in many lands, I finally succeeded in 1978 at Havana, Cuba—a 96 pound Atlantic blue marlin. At that time Jack Samson was Editor-In-Chief of *Field & Stream* magazine. I wrote a story for his February 1979 issue entitled "The Grand Slam of Billfishing—on a Fly Rod"—then six species of billfish.

In 1992 it was Jack Samson's turn to do me one better. By August of that year he had caught all of my six on a fly and went on to take a Pacific blue marlin of 176 pounds on 20 pound tippet at Cabo San Lucas, Mexico. The Grand Slam now stands at seven billfish species for Jack.

I am proud to have helped Jack in the beginning with the basics of this sport and to have fished with him as he learned. It's a pleasure to pen this foreword to the chronicle that Jack is so eminently qualified to present in *Billfish on a Fly*.

Billy Pate
June 26, 1994
Islamorada, Florida

PREFACE

Jack Samson (left) and Billy Pate.

For years I tried to interest publishers in putting out a book about catching billfish on a fly. None thought there would be any market for such a book.

So I am eternally grateful to Frank Amato—truly a man of vision—for realizing there is a great story in the history of fishing for billfish on a fly. He also saw the market for such a book in a whole new generation of young saltwater fly rodders who see a great challenge in taking these big, fast game fish with a fly.

People like Billy Pate and Dr. Webster Robinson fascinated me back in the early 1970s when I read about their catches of sailfish and marlin on a fly rod. I had been catching billfish for years on conventional tackle and had been doing the big game tournament circuit from Florida and the Bahamas to Hawaii and Mexico.

It was great fun, but after I caught a 1,000-plus pound Pacific black marlin with Captain Jeffrey Ferguson aboard the *Reef Hunter* of Cairns, Australia on 80 pound tackle in 1980, the challenge went out of the sport for me. Also I suddenly realized that these great fighting fish really didn't stand much of a chance on today's highly sophisticated big game tackle.

I contacted Billy Pate in Islamorada, Florida—with whom I had been tarpon tournament fishing for years—and asked him to show me the ropes. He was more than gracious—as he always is with people asking for advice—and agreed to take me fishing for sailfish.

I went with him on the first billfish fly fishing tournament out of Islamorada, Florida in 1981. The weather was terrible and we sloshed around the Gulfstream all day while no fish came up. The next day was no better, but at least I got to learn how Billy handled his heavy fly gear and what to do when sailfish come up to a teaser bait. Rip MacIntosh from Palm Beach won that tournament with one sailfish, but at least I had an idea what to do.

In the next several years I caught a few small sailfish off the Florida coast, but never really had a chance to try for anything else. I was Editor-In-Chief of *Field & Stream* in those years and the magazine took up a great deal of my time. I had to live in New York City and the big game fishing stinks in that area.

It was not until I retired from that fine old publication and moved back to my home state of New Mexico in 1983 that I finally found time to go big game fishing again. I would go to Costa Rica and meet Billy and we would fish from places like Flamingo in the north, Bahia Pez Vela and Quepos. We caught a lot of Pacific sailfish on a fly and I began to get better at it.

In the late 1980s I fished at Mazatlan with Jerry Jergens and caught a lot more sailfish, at Golfito in southern Costa Rica with Ed Beattie, Panama with Cam Sigler and Cabo San Lucas with Didier Van der Veecken. I was still catching plenty of Pacific sailfish, but marlin were getting away too often. They were just too strong, fast and big for the 12-weight fly rods I was using.

It wasn't until my partner, Joe Hudson of Islamorada, and I won the first International Invitational Billfish Fly Tournament in Costa Rica in 1989 that I realized we needed stronger and better fly rods if we were going to lift marlin up from the depths with any degree of success.

Joe Fisher, president of the venerable Fisher Rod Company of Nevada, fished with me off Mazatlan, Mexico in 1990 and we conceived the idea of building heavier "lifting" fly rods—rather than the conventional fly-casting ones that had been advertised for sailfish for years.

Joe built a 15-weight, three-piece, graphite fly rod he called his Bluewater Rod and later went up to an 18-weight rod for people who wanted to catch big sharks and tuna on a fly. I never found it necessary to use the 18-weight, but the 15-weight rod was perfect for me.

I went on to land bigger Pacific sailfish faster than I ever had before and—with the advent of the new International Game Fish Association 20 pound tippet class—began to fight marlin longer than before. I had caught a small 43 pound Atlantic blue marlin off Jamaica in 1983 on a 12-weight fly rod and a white cork popper Billy Pate had given me, but because of the small size I really didn't consider it anything to brag about. Even though it was only the second Atlantic blue marlin to be caught on a fly at that time, it was really a tiny fish. Pate had caught the first one off Cuba in 1978—a big blue of 96 pounds—plus a 146 pound striped marlin in 1970 off Ecuador, an 80 pound Atlantic white marlin off Venezuela in 1975 and a 46 pound, 4 ounce Pacific black marlin off Australia in 1972. He was the first man to do this and all his fish were I.G.F.A. world records on a fly. I was certainly not competing with him at that time.

But as the years wore on I got better at the sport—and luckier. I wasn't interested in setting I.G.F.A. world records—preferring to release the fish alive. Like the late, great Lee Wulff, I believe a great game fish is too valuable to be caught only once. However I wanted to be able to say I had caught all the species of sailfish and marlin with a fly.

I knew I would have to document all these fish with witnesses and photographs because there are always "doubting Thomases" who accuse one of making the whole thing up, so I began to document the catches and send them to Mike Leech, director of I.G.F.A.—who compiled them into a file.

I had already caught three small Atlantic sailfish off Florida years before, but had never photographed them or documented them. I had also caught a lot of Pacific sailfish (somewhere between 80 and 90 by 1994) but I caught a big one off Bahia Pez Vela, Costa Rica on June 10th, 1988 that I thought might break Bob Stearn's then-world record—which was somewhere around 112 pounds. It weighed 105, but was not enough to beat Stearns. I was fishing with New Mexico trout guide Chuck Rizuto and two Texans, John Uhr and Deedee Harkins. We photographed the big fish and weighed it. It was caught on a 16 pound tippet.

In August 1990 I had a chance to fish with Captain Calvin Tilley of the *Seaducer* off Townsville, Australia. He only had two days free and by a streak of luck I caught an approximately 50 pound black marlin on a blue and white, double-hooked billfish fly designed by Joe Butorac of Washington state. I was fishing with two Australians—Ian Miller the well-known rod-builder and an Australian outdoor writer named Steve Starling. The little black was photographed and released—with a tag in it.

I caught an approximately 65 pound Atlantic white marlin while fishing off Venezuela in the fall of 1990 with Chuck Rizuto—who had the bad luck of losing a small Atlantic blue marlin when his rod broke. We photographed and released my white—caught on 16 pound tippet.

Because I had never documented any Atlantic sailfish, I caught a big, (for Atlantic sails) approximately 60 pound sail on that same trip to Venezuela with Rizuto and we photographed and released it the same day. It was also caught on a 16 pound tippet.

Realizing my little 43 pound Jamaica marlin was certainly not a representative Atlantic blue, (and I had not documented it anyway—even though we photographed it) I set out to catch a legitimate Atlantic blue marlin on a fly.

I had the chance on May 30, 1992 when Captain Wes Ruggles invited me to fish aboard his outboard-powered 23-foot Seacraft *El Picante* out of the lovely port of Puerto Aventuras on the east coast of Mexico. I caught and released an approximately 65 pound Atlantic blue marlin that took one of my own balao flies and put on a terrific display before being boated. The fish was released and Wes photographed it—along with mate Butch Buie. It was caught on a 20 pound tippet.

Cam Sigler, of Vashon Island, Washington, and I fished

for five days out of Spa Buena Vista Resort on the east coast of Baja California and on July 11, 1992 I hooked and landed an approximately 100 pound Pacific striped marlin on 20 pound tippet after an hour-long battle. The fight was shortened by the Fisher 15-weight Bluewater Rod that helped pump it up from the depths. The fish was photographed and released.

I suddenly realized I was tied with the great Billy Pate—with both sailfish and four species of marlin! Billy realized it too and we both began trying to catch the elusive Pacific blue marlin—the final marlin needed to make a Grand Slam.

I had an approximately 400 pound blue marlin on for about 45 minutes off Tropic Star Lodge in Panama in February 1992, but it broke me off. I lost another off Mazatlan that winter and Billy—fishing off Quepos, Costa Rica—had an approximately 400 pound blue marlin on for 7 1/2 hours before having to cut it off at dark—miles out to sea.

In August of 1992, Eric Heimpel, owner of the Star Fleet in Cabo San Lucas, called me to say he had a cancellation and had four open days on the boat *Elinor*. I flew down and fished with Captain Martin Gonzales, mate Guillermo Estrada and Jerry Cevallos, manager of Star Fleet. On the morning of August 17, 1992 I hooked and boated a 176 pound Pacific blue marlin that took one of my own dorado flies on a 20 pound tippet. The fish was brought ashore, weighed by I.G.F.A. representative Luis Bulnes at Cabo San Lucas and photographed.

Over the nine years it took to catch the Atlantic and Pacific sailfish and all five species of marlin I was helped and encouraged by a lot of people. It would be impossible to name them all, but these stand out: Billy Pate, Bill Barnes, Joe Hudson, John Uhr, Deedee Harkins, Chuck Rizuto, Ed Beattie, Didier Van der Veecken, Bob Nauheim, George Hommell, Cam Sigler, Brian Peterson, Joe Fisher, Nick Curcione, Steve Sloan, Mike Leech, the late Elwood "E.K." Harry, Ted Juracsik, Calvin Tilley, Eric and Bill Heimpel, Jerry Jergens, Wes Ruggles, Martin Gonzales, Jerry Cevallos, Terri Kitteridge, Leon Chandler, Chuy Valdez, Luis Bulnes, Scott Forrestal, Steve Abel, Don Drown, Terry Baird, Mark Tupper, George Cook, Gilberto Aviles, Jack Erskine, Juan Arismendi, Jimmy Nix, Mike Sakamoto, Stu Apte, Chet Young, Dan Baumgartner, John Kolman, Tom Bradwell, Winston Moore, Pathways, American Airlines, Trey Combs, Tim Choate, Cherri Jergens, Ken Carmen, Dave Sylvester, Pat Ford, Ed Draper, Frontiers, Rick Gaffney, Denton Hill, Jake Jordan, Jim Kenyon, Dave Lear, Colin Moore, Ezio Maruhashi, Kentaro Amagai, Joe Saracione, Jack Charlton, LACSA Airlines, John Barr and Don Tompkins.

Jack Samson

CHAPTER

1

Fly Fishing's Ultimate Sport

While sailfish and marlin have been successfully caught for decades on both heavy and light conventional tackle, the taking of billfish on a fly rod is a relatively new sport.

The practice is catching on world-wide with astonishing popularity—perhaps because the fly rod has been restricted to small freshwater game fish like trout, salmon and bass for centuries. Saltwater fly fishing in general is the fastest-growing segment of fly fishing, but the pursuit of large saltwater species has caught the imagination of the general angling public in the last few decades. Billfish are enticed to the surface with generally the same baits and lures that they are in conventional big game fishing, but the baits are hookless. When a billfish attacks the trolled baits, they are pulled rapidly away and a fly is then cast to the searching fish. Surprisingly, to many fly rodders, billfish take a fly as eagerly as many smaller game fish species. The major difference is that—when hooked—billfish are far stronger and faster than most saltwater game fish.

Fly shops carrying saltwater fly fishing tackle have been deluged with questions about the proper rods, reels, lines, leaders, flies and knots needed to take these fast and powerful big game fish on the long rods. And, unfortunately, not all of these shops have either the right tackle in stock or the knowledge necessary to instruct the beginner in this new and fascinating sport. It is certainly not the fault of the fly shops, tackle stores or the tackle industry. The sudden burst of interest in the sport took everyone by surprise—including those of us who had been doing it for decades. Perhaps the very uniqueness of it—hooking, fighting and boating such giant fish on relatively flimsy fly tackle—contributed to it suddenly being the thing to try in saltwater fly fishing.

Fortunately for the novice, there are a few companies that saw the sport coming and were able to design strong enough

Above: **Lee Cuddy and the first record sailfish caught on a fly—a 47 pound fish caught off Florida June 4, 1964.** *Right:* **Washington state's veteran fly fisherman Cam Sigler and a big Pacific sailfish he caught on a fly in Pinas Bay, Panama.**

Left: **The late pioneering salt water fly rodder Harry Kime and his "Tuttie-Frutie" sailfish fly.** *Middle:* **Veteran big game fly fisherman Bill Barnes and a big Pacific sail caught on a fly off Flamingo, Costa Rica.** *Right:* **Expert saltwater fly rodder Stu Apte and his world record 136 pound Pacific sailfish caught June 25, 1965 in Pinas Bay, Panama. It is still a 12 pound tippet record at this writing.**

fly rods, and reels with the proper drag and enough line capacity to handle these giant fish. Line companies have come up with heavy and strong enough lines to hold billfish and leader material is now equal to the task of containing big fish in abrasive saltwater.

The I.G.F.A.—having watched the phenomenal growth in the sport of fly fishing for big ocean fish in the past few decades—anticipated the need for a stronger tippet class than the existing 2, 4, 6, 8, 12, and 16 pound categories, and introduced the new 20 pound class tippet—effective April 1, 1991.

It seems hard to believe, time-wise, but the first Pacific sail entered for an I.G.F.A. record was one caught by Stu Apte at Pinas Bay, Panama on June 25, 1965—still a record today.

While Doc Robinson's was the first striped marlin caught on a fly, the late Lee Wulff—a true pioneer in the field of saltwater fly fishing—entered a 148 pound striped marlin for an I.G.F.A. record on 12 pound tippet. The fish was caught in May, 1967 off Salinas, Ecuador and is listed as a 12 pound tippet record as of this writing.

According to Lefty Kreh, who certainly should know, the first record sailfish caught on a fly was an Atlantic sailfish of 47 pounds caught by Lee Cuddy off Florida on June 4, 1964.

Billy Pate's Atlantic blue remained an I.G.F.A. world record until 1990 when Jim Gray of Islamorada, Florida caught a 159 pound blue off St. Thomas in the Virgin Islands on 16 pound tippet.

Charlie Tombras of Knoxville, Tennessee submitted to the I.G.F.A. a 208 pound Atlantic blue marlin he caught on a fly May 20, 1994 off La Guaira Bank, Venezuela. The big blue was caught on a 20 pound tippet. That is now a new record.

Small Pacific black marlin are the perfect size for the saltwater fly rodder as they run from about 50-100 pounds in the vicinity of Cairns and Cape Bowling Green off the Queensland coast of Australia. Pate was the first to catch them in 1972—fish of 46 pounds, 4 ounces; 38 pounds, 10 ounces and 42 pounds, 6 ounces on 6, 12 and 15 pound tippet.

Pate's former wife, Laura, caught a 38 pound black on 10 pound test tippet on September 14, 1972—to become a world record in the old records kept by the Saltwater Fly Rodders of America—before I.G.F.A. began to keep such records. Another woman, Delores Williams, former wife of baseball star Ted Williams, caught a 68 pound white marlin on a fly in September of 1975 at La Guiara, Venezuela. She did not enter it for a record.

In the late 1960s and early 1970s, those of us who began experimenting with fly rods for billfish started out using both the conventional floating and sinking 90 foot fly line. But the length and diameter of these lines proved unsatisfactory. They put up such a resistance to the water when a billfish was jumping that the fragile tippets parted. It was finally decided that the best system was to use very short, 25-30 foot, fast-sinking shooting heads because their weight made them easier to cast and their small diameter cut down on water resistance.

Professor Charles O. Mather, in his excellent book *Billfish*, wrote that scientists have estimated billfish can reach top speeds of 50-70 miles per hour. At that speed, a fish weighing over 100 pounds puts tremendous pressure on line, leader and backing. In order to reduce this pressure and sudden shock from speeding billfish, most of us

12 pound tippet. I caught a white on a fly October 23, 1990 off La Guaira, Venezuela that was about 60 pounds. I released it and have only the photo to remember that great fish by, but it would not have weighed enough to challenge Pate's fish on 16 pound tippet.

Earlier, Judge W.O. Mehrtens, caught a 58 pound, 8 ounce white marlin off Venezuela on September 30, 1976.

Californian Ray Beadle caught two Pacific black marlin off Australia in 1987 to beat Pate's 12 pound and 16 pound tippet records—fish of 85 pounds, 15

decided a length of stretchable mono running line would be a good idea somewhere in the terminal tackle. Nowadays most big game fly fishermen use a 100 foot section of 30-45 pound soft mono between the backing and the fly line. There are a number of good monos around for this purpose—the best being Cortland 30 pound Cobra and 40 pound Plion I and an excellent soft, highly-stretchable 45 pound test mono from West Germany called Schneider. It is difficult to find, but I managed to get some from that excellent saltwater fly fisherman and tackle designer, Jack Erskine of Cairns, Australia.

Pate was the first angler to catch a record Atlantic white marlin on a fly—an 80 pound fish that was boated September 17, 1975 off Venezuela and taken on 16 pound tippet. It is still a world record.

Floridian Pat Ford set the 8 pound tippet class record with a 73 pound fish taken off Venezuela on September 22, 1984. Andrew MacGrath caught a 74 pound, 8 ounce white on November 17, 1988 to set the I.G.F.A record for

ounces and 94 pounds, 3 ounces.

Florida's Jim Gray caught four blue marlin that set world records: his 159 pound Atlantic blue from the Virgin Islands and another Atlantic blue from San Salvador, Bahamas that weighed 113 pounds, 4 ounces and was caught on a 20 pound tippet August 5, 1993. In addition he has caught two Pacific blue marlin on a fly—a 203 pound, 8 ounce fish from Guanamar, Costa Rica caught February 12, 1991 on 16 pound tippet and a big 260 pound Pacific blue marlin caught August 6, 1991 at Flamingo, Costa Rica on 20 pound tippet.

Andrew MacGrath caught a 74 pound, 8 ounce white marlin at Vitoria, Santos, Brazil on November 17, 1988 and Leo Cloostermaans caught a 73 pound white at Horta Faial, Azores on August 14, 1993 to set a world record on 20 pound tippet.

Diane Harbaugh of Islamorada, Florida is the first woman to catch an Atlantic blue marlin on a fly. She caught the 93 pound marlin off the Turks and Caicos Islands in July of 1994.

Top left: **Author Jack Samson and a big fly-caught Pacific sailfish landed in Pinas Bay, Panama (released).** *Top right:* **Lee's Ferry Anglers' Wendy Hanvold and her 136 pound world record Pacific striped marlin—caught on 20 pound tippet in December, 1993 off the Socorro Islands.** *Bottom Left:* **The late saltwater fly fishing pioneer Lee Wulff and his 136 pound Pacific striped marlin—caught on 12 pound tippet in May of 1967 off Salinas, Ecuador. It is still a world record as of this writing.** *Bottom right:* **Californian Denton Hill and his bad-luck 174 lb Pacific striped marlin he caught on a 16 pound tippet July 20, 1990 off Costa Rica. Because all he had was a wired-down flying gaff aboard, the I.G.F.A disallowed his catch.**

Guaita Daniele caught a 34 pound, 2 ounce black marlin off Cairns, Australia on a fly August 27, 1993 to set a world record in the 20 pound tippet category.

Californian Denton Hill would have set a new world record for Pacific striped marlin had it not been for a bad break. On July 20, 1990 he was fishing out of El Ocotal, Costa Rica when he hooked, fought and boated a big 174 pound striped marlin on a 16 pound tippet. The only long-handled gaff aboard was one with a detachable head that was securely wrapped with 100 pound mono so that it could not come off. Nevertheless the I.G.F.A ruled that it could not be accepted as a world record because it was a flying gaff—wrapped or not. The fish would have beaten the weights of both Lee Wulff's and Billy Pate's striped marlin.

In December of 1993, on one of the long-range boat trips to the Socorro Islands, Ray Beadle caught a 105 pound and a 109 pound Pacific striped marlin, and Thomas & Thomas Rod Company's veteran billfish fly rodder Brian Peterson caught a 105 pound, 6 ounce striped marlin on 20 pound tippet—which was certified by the I.G.F.A. But all three striped marlin were defeated in the 20 pound tippet class by a 136 pound striped marlin caught by Lee's Ferry Anglers' Wendy Hanvold on the same trip.

West Coast angler Ed Rice caught an 88 pound Pacific striped marlin off Cabo San Lucas, Mexico in December 1985—while fishing with expert fly rodder Didier Van der Veecken.

The Pacific blue marlin has long evaded the saltwater fly rodder. There are two reasons: It generally runs to weights that might be too much to handle on a fly rod and it is very difficult to find an area where the blues are concentrated. I lost three of them in a three-year period—one at Mazatlan, Panama, and Cabo San Lucas—before finally catching a 176 pound fish off Cabo in 1992. Cabo San Lucas is the best place to try for Pacific blue marlin that run from approximately 150-250 pounds.

That intrepid fly rod experimenter, Mike Sakamoto of Hawaii, caught a huge 206 pound Pacific blue marlin a decade ago using a prototype 14-weight fly rod designed by Tim Grennan. Mike was trolling (prohibited by I.G.F.A rules for record fish) a fly he designed himself called The Bag Lady. It sported a 10/0 Mustad hook and a body made from surfboard foam. It took Mike hours to land that marlin but he did it—not to submit it for an I.G.F.A record, but just to prove it could be done; it was the very first caught on a fly rod.

While some of these fish were caught on standard 12-13-weight graphite fly rods (except Sakamoto's) the trend from now on will be toward a new family of "lifting" fly rods that are being developed by rod companies for anglers in search of big fish fly rod records—using the 20 pound tippet. The companies pioneering these powerful rods are J. Kennedy Fisher, Sage, Loomis and Thomas &

Thomas—so far.

Some of the early sailfish fly records were impressive. C.A. Peacock, Jr. caught a 49 pound, 8 ounce Atlantic sail off Cozumel, Mexico on April 13, 1975 on 10 pound tippet, and John Emery caught a 55 pound, 8 ounce sail off the same place on April 17, 1977 on 12 pound tippet to set a record.

On the Pacific sailfish scene Flip Pallot caught an impressive 102 pound, 12 ounce sail on August 11, 1973 to set a record on 10 pound tippet and Gil Drake took a monster 115 pound Pacific sail July 25, 1967, at El Coco, Costa Rica on 15 pound tippet. Stu Apte's giant 136 pound Pacific sail, taken on a fly June 25, 1965 at Pinas Bay, Panama, is still a world record on 12 pound tippet.

Rufus Wakeman, that excellent fly rodder from Jensen Beach, Florida, set two sailfish world records—a 12 pound tippet record with a 65 pound, 9 ounce Atlantic sailfish from Dakar, Senegal on June 26, 1988 and a phenomenal catch of a 76 pound, 12 ounce Pacific sailfish caught February 1, 1989 off Golfito, Costa Rica on a 4 pound tippet!

Two other records were set in 1989 for Pacific sailfish. Jim Watt broke Billy Pate's 8 pound test record with a 98 pound, 4 ounce sail caught April 29th while fishing out of that fine big game resort, Bahia Pez Vela in Costa Rica. Excellent fly fisherman, Eizo Maruhashi of Japan—who has placed far up in the three International Billfish Fly Tournaments held at Flamingo Beach, Costa Rica, and sponsored by World Wide Sportsman, Inc, of Islamorada, Florida—broke Bob Stearns long-standing 16 pound tippet record for Pacific sailfish with a whopping 124 pound sail caught July 21, 1989 off Costa Rica.

Veteran fly angler Charlie Owen set two world records for Atlantic sailfish with a 31 pound sail caught April 1, 1989 at Cozumel on 4 pound tippet and a 71 pound, 8 ounce sail caught at the same place May 10, 1990 on 8 pound tippet.

Jim Gray took two big Pacific sailfish for records in 1991 at Quepos, Costa Rica—a 94 pound, 8 ounce fish on 4 pound tippet and a 106 pound, 8 ounce sail on an 8 pound tippet.

Lee J. Dixon, II caught a whopping 128 pound, 8 ounce Pacific sailfish January 10, 1993 at Quepos on 20 pound tippet to set a new world record.

Hugh Vincent caught two Atlantic sailfish for records—an 83 pound fish on September 17, 1992 on 16 pound tippet and a 102 pound sail on October 22, 1993 on 20 pound tippet—both at Principe Island.

Why have so many new records been set and so many old ones topped in the last decade? The answer lies in a combination of improved tackle and a growing awareness of and an interest in the sport—fed by increased space devoted to it in the outdoor press. There were a few pioneers—Winston Moore and anglers like the late Harry Kime of California—who had been quietly catching sailfish for years. Neither man was interested in setting records, but simply in catching the fish on flies. Moore probably caught more than 100 sailfish in his career—much of it in the 1970s—and Kime at least half that many. Kime was an all-around saltwater fly fisherman and tried as much for dorado, yellowtail, roosterfish and tarpon as he did for sailfish and marlin. He did hook a few striped marlin in the Sea of Cortez, but told me he did not think there was much of a chance of saltwater fly rodders landing marlin much above 200 pounds. He would have changed his mind had he seen some of the new fly rods and reels.

Most of the reels used in taking the first sailfish and marlin were the standard tarpon models—the Fin-Nor #4, the venerable Seamaster and Billy Pate's tarpon reel. Most of them had a line capacity of about 400 yards of 30 pound braided Dacron or Micron backing—plus a 90 foot fly line.

But it is in the area of large sailfish and marlin reels that big changes have been made. Billy Pate Reels (produced by design engineer Ted Juracsik) came out with a marlin model with a capacity of 600 yards of 30 pound backing and a slick anti-reverse drag system. That was quickly followed by one from California engineer and fly fisherman Steve Abel who produced the Abel #5 direct-drive fly reel with a capacity of 900 yards of 30 pound backing plus a fly line. I have caught both sailfish and marlin on both reels and they are excellent. Both Fin-Nor and Seamaster make excellent marlin reels and Charlton builds a fine sailfish reel.

Fly lines are no problem with sailfish and marlin on a fly rod as two companies—Cortland and Scientific Angler/3M—have been refining their saltwater lines for years. They have been producing excellent fly lines for tarpon fishermen—which hold up well in saltwater. They are now making billfish lines that test out at about 45 pounds breaking strength—plenty strong enough.

Leader material and mono running line are salt-resistant and come in both soft and hard brands for tippet sections and shock leader. I have found Mason hard mono to be good for class tippet sections as it is very hard and resists

cuts and nicks.

Most billfish fly fishermen—like me—made their own sailfish and marlin flies years ago because there were no commercial fly tiers making flies for fish that big. Billy Pate designed the original double-hooked billfish streamer fly—with white saddle hackles—that became the standard fly for sailfish and marlin. I make my own double-hooked billfish flies imitating bait fish. Few companies market them commercially.

Knots are of the utmost importance in billfish fly fishing. There is some latitude in choosing which knots to use, but not much. One needs knots of 100 percent strength for this kind of fishing.

What size billfish can we expect to catch in the near future with the improved rods, reels and the new 20 pound tippet class? It is anyone's guess, but I wager we will start catching marlin in the 300-400 pound class before too many years. Why not? The rods will take the strain, the reels will have the line capacity and the 20 pound tippet is quite strong. Peter Mahood of Australia caught a 1,050 pound Pacific black marlin off Cairns in 1976 on 20 pound mono—exactly the same strength as our new tippet class!

Winston Moore, truly a great pioneer saltwater fly fisherman, who has caught more than 100 Pacific sailfish on a fly during his long career. He did not turn any in for records.

CHAPTER

2

Best Places For Billfish on a Fly

It is not enough for fly rodders to know where billfish are going to be at any time of the year. They have to know where the *right* sailfish or marlin will be.

Unlike conventional big game fishermen, fly rodders are limited to billfish, generally, up to about 300 pounds. Nobody has yet caught a 300 pound billfish on a fly—to my knowledge anyway—but it is only a matter of time before someone does. The I.G.F.A fly rod record so far is a 260 pound Pacific blue marlin—on 20 pound class tippet, but no one knows how many larger marlin have been caught by anglers who don't care about records and release their fish.

Today we are limited only by skill and luck—mostly luck. We have the rods, reels, lines, leaders and flies to catch larger billfish.

In looking for sailfish and marlin in sizes that average about 100-350 pounds, the selection of locations is somewhat limited. It is no problem holding sailfish below 200 pounds. The biggest sail on record for a fly rod is still 136 pounds—caught almost 30 years ago on a 12 pound tippet, but there again, no one knows how many bigger sails have been caught by fly rodders who prefer not to kill their fish and turn them loose.

But marlin are a different ball game. There would be little sense, for example, in fishing with a fly rod off Cairns, Australia in October or November for black marlin—where 1,000 pound blacks are common and the average black runs somewhere in the 500-600 pound category. On the other hand, if one wanted to catch a nice fly rod black marlin, one would be wise to fish off Townsville, Australia—inside the reef—in August or September. The blacks

The excellent harbor of Flamingo, Costa Rica.

18

BILLFISH ON A FLY

average 50-100 pounds then.

White marlin almost never get much larger than 100 pounds so it doesn't much matter where one fishes for them for most of the year. They can be caught all up and down the Atlantic coast from late spring until late summer, but to find them in great numbers, one needs to go to Venezuela in October and November. A month later they can be found concentrated off Brazil.

Atlantic sailfish are no problem to find—congregating off the Florida east coast—particularly in the winter off such areas as the Jupiter Inlet and Palm Beach. But they are also found to be plentiful off the Florida Keys at that time and later in the spring. Cozumel in March is a fine spot for Atlantic sails—plus white marlin and small Atlantic blue marlin—up through May.

Places where one might catch small Atlantic blue marlin are few in number, but if I were to advise a beginner where to go I would suggest Jamaica in February and March, St. Thomas later in the spring and summer and Venezuela in October, November and early December.

Pacific sailfish range all the way up the west coast of Central and South America to Baja and the Sea of Cortez. I have not fished Colombia, but some of the booking people claim there are several good fishing ports on the west coast. But the reports of kidnapping have kept me from fishing there and I figure the farther away I am from the drug scene the better off I am.

If I were to name the best place to catch Pacific sailfish at any one time, I would recommend Panama in April and May—particularly from a lodge such as Tropic Star on Pinas Bay. After that I would fish from such spots as Bahia Pez Vela on the upper coast of Costa Rica and slightly after that, Flamingo in the spring. During the winter months—when the winds make fishing almost impossible in those northern areas—I'd fish Golfito in extreme southern Costa Rica and at Quepos, where a barrier range of mountains keep the winds down and the seas calm.

In Mexico, in the spring, Mazatlan would be my first choice for sailfish—starting from about May and lasting on through October. That is on the mainland, but off Baja there are plenty of sails in the late spring and summer months from an area south of La Paz all the way up to Loreto and Mulege.

Surprisingly enough—though most fly rodders think the only place one can find black marlin small enough for a fly

rod is off Australia—there are small black marlin off Panama in January, February and March. Off the mouth of Pinas Bay they run in the 300-500 pound range during those months and are caught on a regular basis by conventional big game anglers and light tackle fisherman. I have not had a chance to try for them yet on a fly, but plan to in the future.

The acrobatic Pacific striped marlin is a natural for fly rodders. It seldom runs over 150 pounds—which is just right. If I had to choose where to go to get striped marlin on a fly, I'd pick the East Cape of Baja—from about La Paz down to Cabo San Lucas from May to October.

Another excellent spot for striped marlin is off Ecuador in the spring—out of the port of Salinas—though it is a difficult place to reach. Striped marlin are caught regularly off Panama and Costa Rica, but there is really no one spot where they congregate at any one time. I have fished for them a lot off Mazatlan in February, March and April and have found them resting on the surface in small pods in each of those months.

The resort owners in New Zealand tell me they catch striped marlin regularly in the 250 pound category, but I have never gone there to try for them on a fly. Looking at the I.G.F.A *World Record Game Fishes*, one can see that the weights of striped marlin caught in New Zealand on conventional tackle certainly are impressive—271, 494, 398, 423, 414—exciting sizes to a fly rodder!

The Pacific blue marlin is the tough one. Unfortunately there is really no one place you can be certain of finding blue marlin in any great numbers at any one time. I fished for them for years from Panama, Costa Rica, the west coast of Mexico and off Baja and I would have to say the best place to try for them would be out of Cabo San Lucas. There are Pacific blue marlin in Hawaii and at a number of Pacific islands, but in such sizes that they would be impractical for a fly rodder.

El Nino notwithstanding, the best time for them off Baja would be from late spring up through November. And while there is no guarantee they would be the right size for fly fishermen, looking at the catch records out of Cabo would indicate that more blue marlin in the 200-400 pound category are caught there than anywhere else.

Unfortunately I have seen blues hanging on the scales at Cabo as small as 60-70 pounds—which indicates they migrate past that port at a fairly early age.

Above: **The beautiful Spa Buena Vista resort on Baja's East Cape—haven for striped marlin, sailfish and Pacific blue marlin.** *Facing page top:* **The harbor at Cabo San Lucas—a prime billfish spot—at the tip of the Baja Penninsula.** *Facing page bottom:* **The beautiful resort of Tropic Star Lodge on Panama's Pinas Bay—marvelous spot for sailfish, Pacific striped marlin, blue marlin and fly rod-size black marlin.**

3

Mazatlan Sailfish on a Fly

"There is no way you are going to convince me this is a sport that is catching on," Jerry Jergens said as we churned through the calm Pacific sea after leaving the sheltered port of Mazatlan on the west coast of Mexico.

"I've been catching sailfish and marlin off this coast since I was a little kid," he went on as I put together the four-piece, 12-weight graphite fly rod. "And though I've caught sails and a lot of striped marlin using 20 pound mono on level-winding gear, I doubt if anyone can do it on a fly rod. A fly rod!" he continued, "Cripes, I've been catching trout on a fly rod in Wyoming and Montana every summer with my parents and I've lost a lot of big *trout* on a fly rod. And you're trying to tell me you can hold a 100 pound sail on a fly rod—and maybe a 150 pound marlin?"

Jerry was born in Mexico City, but now lives in New Braunfels, Texas—a suburb of San Antonio. An avid hunter and fisherman, he operates Mazatlan Sportsman, an outfitting service catering to sportsmen who want to fish for largemouth bass, hunt doves and waterfowl and fish for billfish near Mazatlan.

"Pass me that reel bag," I said, sliding a 5 foot-long leader from a plastic envelope and taking a white, double-hooked popper from the tackle box.

"This here?" Jerry asked, handing me the cloth bag. "Wow, that's a really big fly reel. How much line does it hold?"

"Six hundred yards of 30 pound Micron backing—plus a 30 foot weight-forward sinking shooting head and 100 feet of 35 pound mono," I said, attaching the heavy reel to the rod.

Facing page: **A fly-hooked Pacific striped marlin leaps from the sea off Mazatlan, Mexico.** *Above:* **Jerry Jergens fights a big sailfish off Mazatlan.**

"What do you need 100 feet of mono for?" Jerry asked.

"To give me some stretch in the terminal tackle," I said, running the fly line through the rod guides. "If I fastened the fly line directly to the backing—which has very little stretch factor—it would be easier for the fish to break the 16 pound class tippet."

"Why don't you use a regular 90 foot floating fly line instead of a short, sinking shooting head," he asked.

"For the same reason," I said, fastening the loop of the leader section to the loop of the 40 pound butt leader. "With these big fish traveling at such speeds through the water, there is too much resistance from a thick, 90 foot floating fly line. The short length and the small diameter of the sinking shooting head present less resistance to the water."

Jerry nodded gravely as I tied the white 5/0-hooked popper to the 1 foot of 100 pound mono shock leader with a 3 1/2-times clinch knot—as the boat suddenly slowed down. Jerry stood up.

"Here we are," he said, stretching in the warmth of the June morning. "What do you want me to do—stand by with the camera?"

"I want you to work, Jergens, not loaf around in the morning sunlight," I said. "See that long teaser rod stuck in the starboard gunwale? With that rod we tease the billfish up close to the boat so I can cast this fly to them. Take one of those small mackerel we rigged up without a hook in it and tie it to the swivel at the end of the line on that rod. Run it back about a hundred feet behind the boat."

"What happens when a fish hits it—without a hook?"

"That's exactly the point," I said. "With no hook in it, the sailfish can't get hooked by it. What you do is reel the bait in just ahead of the sailfish's bill. Keep it away from him until it gets to about 30-40 feet from the boat. Then you yank it away from him and I'll cast the fly to it—but," I added, "The captain has to take the boat out of gear at the same time I cast the fly. It's International Game Fish Association rules—for fish that are submitted for a record."

"In neutral, why?" Jerry asked.

"Because, Jerry," I said, "It is next to impossible to catch a sailfish or marlin by trolling a fly. These fish have hard, thorny bills and they will keep whacking away at the fly if the boat is moving—and never get hooked. If the boat slows down or stops, the billfish can take the fly and turn away with it in its mouth—giving me a chance to set the hook in the soft corner of the mouth—got it?"

"Got it," Jerry said. "How does the captain know when to stop?"

"That's your job, my Spanish-speaking chum. When I start to cast, you yell up at him to stop—in Spanish."

"I'll say 'alto' to him then." Jerry said.

"Good," I said, moving to the right-hand corner of the cockpit where I began to strip some line from the reel into an empty plastic bucket on the deck. It was to keep my line coiled in the bottom so it wouldn't become tangled in the cockpit. The port outrigger was not being used in order to give me backcasting room.

The mate had run out a big hookless Kona head teaser on the starboard outrigger—about 100 feet back—and also a "daisy chain" of five hookless plastic squids on a flat line close to the transom. It would be his duty to bring in both these teasers when billfish came up—leaving to Jerry the job of luring the fish in with the fresh fish teaser bait.

"Assuming you're lucky enough to hook a sail." Jerry said, standing by the teaser rod, "Are you sure that fly rod will handle it?"

"It's handled a dozen Pacific sails so far—and two striped marlin," I said. "A 9 foot, 12-weight graphite fly rod can handle a lot of fish."

"I'll believe it when I see it," Jerry muttered to himself.

It was nearly an hour before a sailfish came up for the baits. We had spotted two on the surface, but they had decided not to feed.

"Pez Vela!"—sailfish—the captain shouted from above. I saw the tip of the dorsal fin and the bill as the fish slashed at the bright orange plastic of the Kona head on the outrigger. The mate grabbed a rod from the starboard gunwale holders jerked the line from the outrigger clip and began reeling the lure in rapidly. Jerry grabbed the 10 foot long teaser rod and stood—holding it ready.

A striped marlin basks in the sun on the surface off Mexico's west coast.

The sailfish, losing site of the Kona head, switched its attention to the rigged mackerel at the end of Jerry's line. It began slashing at the bait.

"Bring it in slowly—just ahead of its bill," I shouted, picking up the fly rod and dropping the fly into the water behind the moving boat. I let about 20 feet of line out of the rod tip in preparation for a backcast. The mate—his Kona head lure safely in—grabbed the flat line and quickly stripped in the squids.

Jerry had brought the sailfish within about 40 feet of the transom—where it was trying to eat the rigged mackerel.

"Jerk it away from him," I shouted, "and tell the skipper to stop the engine."

Jerry pointed the tip of the big rod at the fish and gave a mighty heave—at the same time turning his head to look at the captain.

"Alto, alto!" he yelled as the mackerel came sailing into the cockpit. The boat suddenly slowed and began to coast forward. The sailfish was frantically searching for the mackerel bait as I made a quick backcast and dropped the big white popper about 6 feet from the circling sailfish. As I stripped the line with my left hand, the popper chugged noisily on the surface.

The sailfish suddenly engulfed the popper and turned away from the boat with the fly in its mouth. Still holding onto the line with my left hand, I struck hard several times with the big rod—jerking low and to my right. I felt the hooks sink in and the line go taut as the sailfish streaked away.

"Whoooeee!" Jerry screamed as the fish began to thrash.

"Tell the captain to go ahead slowly," I yelled. "I've got to keep slack out of this line."

By this time the sailfish was 100 yards out and still leaping. I held the rod level—tip pointing at the moving fish—and let the fish have line. The drag was set very lightly until the fish had finished its first long, leaping run. After that I could put more tension on the drag in order to pump the fish in.

"I don't believe it!" Jerry shouted, scurrying for his camera, "If I hadn't seen it, I'd never believe it!"

It took 20 minutes to pump the sailfish to the boat. For a while it dove deeply—where it could set its pectoral fins and sulk in the depths. We moved the boat forward slowly and planed the sailfish back up—where it began another series of jumps. Jerry was busy taking photographs as the mate finally grabbed the bill and slid the sailfish over the side.

"Well," I asked. "What do you think of fly fishing for billfish?"

He stood looking at me, shaking his head.

"That is the damndest thing I ever saw!" he said. "What do I think? Give me that fly rod and get on that teaser rod. The next sail belongs to me. This is a whole new ball game!"

Top: **Author Samson with a big fly-caught Pacific sailfish off Mazatlan.** *Bottom:* **The beautiful port city of Mazatlan.**

4

Billfish of Panama

Cam Sigler of Vashon Island, Washington, caught his first sailfish on a fly off Mazatlan, Mexico in November 1990 and it completely changed his life.

Ask his wife, Sue. "Honestly," she said, "He hasn't been the same since. All he wants to do is catch another!"

Cam, who is a veteran trout and salmon fly fisherman and author of *Guide to Fly Fishing*, was delighted when I invited him to accompany me to Tropic Star Lodge in Panama to fly fish for sailfish. Ed Beattie of 5 Star Expeditions had tipped me off to the fishing possibilities.

"In May the lodge has more sailfish than anywhere in the world," he said, "and it's been that way for 30 years that I know of."

It was no exaggeration. There were sailfish everywhere—on the surface, finning in the bright sunlight—and surfacing to our trolled teaser baits. We were fishing in calm seas not more than a quarter-mile offshore from a spectacularly beautiful and rugged coastal mountain range about 100 miles south of Panama City. Pinas Bay, the sheltered home of Tropic Star Lodge, was only a handful of miles to the south of us.

For Cam, it had already been a banner day. A sailfish had come up to our trolled bonito strip baits not an

hour after we began fishing at 7:00 a.m. on a beautiful May morning. The mate, Olivio Cossio quickly reeled in the port bait while I kept the starboard strip bait a foot or so ahead of the fish's searching bill. When the sailfish was not more than 30 feet from the transoms I quickly yanked the strip bait away from the fish and the skipper, Isauro Urrutia slipped the controls of the 31-foot Bertram into neutral.

Above: **A fly-hooked sailfish jumps close to Tropic Star Lodge in Panama.** *Facing page:* **The snug harbor of Tropic Star Lodge in Pinas Bay, Panama.**

Above left: **Author Samson watches a big sailfish tear off hundreds of yards of 30 pound backing.** *Above right:* **Cam gets his sailfish close to the boat.** *Below:* **Cam Sigler fights a big leaping sailfish.**

Cam cast the double-hooked fly about 6 feet from the fish and the sail immediately took the fly. Setting the hooks with a series of quick jerks, Cam raised the rod tip as the big sailfish went skittering away across the calm surface. On my advice he had set the drag on his reel very lightly and the fish was peeling hundreds of yards off the reel as it headed east toward the rugged mountains.

Isauro put the boat into reverse and began to back down quickly. The sailfish had jumped at least a dozen times before slowing down to head for the depths and Cam gradually tightened his drag now that the acrobatics were over. It is during the jumping that a sailfish's bill can whip around and quickly sever the fragile class tippet above the 12 inch 100 pound shock leader. The other dangerous time for a fly rodder is when the billfish is close to the boat at the end of a battle. It can thrash about at the last minute and cut the leader with its rough, serrated bill.

It took about 20 minutes before Cam had the sailfish close to the boat. The fish was down about 200 feet and he had to pump it up slowly. Both Cam and I were experimenting with prototype billfish fly rods. His was a 2-piece, 13-weight Loomis offshore Billfish fly rod designed by world record distance fly caster Steve Rajeff. The rod was holding up admirably under the strain—far better than most of the standard 12-weight fly rods used today for tarpon and sailfish.

The sailfish suddenly decided to come to the surface and jumped several times close to the boat. Cam pointed the tip of his rod at the fish to lessen the strain on the 20 pound tippet and the skipper swung the stern in the direction of the thrashing fish. When the boat backed up to the sailfish, Olivio reached out with a small gaff and hooked it around the bill. He drew the fish close to the stern and Isauro slipped the controls into neutral and jumped down to the cockpit. He quickly donned a pair of cloth gloves and leaned over the side and grabbed the sailfish by the bill. Cam sidestepped quickly as the two men slid the 90-100 pound fish over the gunwale and onto the bait box.

There were handshakes, backslaps and a lot of noise in the cockpit as I photographed Cam's second billfish on a fly. The mate gently slid the big billfish over the side and we watched it swim slowly downward in the clear blue depths.

We were to boat and release two more sailfish that day and lose another half a dozen from pulled-out hooks and broken tippets before heading back to the lodge in mid-afternoon. A fishing day at Tropic Star Lodge runs from about 6 a.m. to 3 p.m.—ending before the big May cumulus cloud buildup in late afternoon which signals the beginning of the Panama rainy season. The rainy season runs from about mid-May to November and the lodge sea-

Above left: **A big sailfish comes aboard. Note the double-hooked sailfish fly on 7/0 hooks is hung-up on the base of the bill.** *Right:* **Author Samson with a big Panama sailfish—just prior to release.** *Bottom:* **The sun rises over a quiet harbor in Pinas Bay.**

son lasts from December 1st to June lst.

Tropic Star Lodge was built in the early 1960s. It was a massive undertaking as every bit of building material and equipment had to be brought into Pinas Bay by barge. Today the luxurious fishing resort is owned and operated by Teri and Mike Andrews. Her father purchased the lodge from the second owners, the Kennedy family, more than a decade ago. The camp operates a fleet of 31 foot Bertram Sportfisherman equipped with twin diesels and can accommodate 18 anglers at a time. It is a first-class fishing operation and the food, lodging and service is unsurpassed anywhere else in the tropics.

Although May is the peak month for sailfish, they are caught year-round just offshore from the lodge. Earlier in the season the offshore fishing grounds are loaded with black, striped and blue marlin. Dorado, tuna, jacks and roosterfish can be caught near the shore. Bait is no problem as the coast is alive with bonito schools and they are caught each morning on a small reef just moments from the lodge.

Cam and I fished for five days and I have never been anywhere with more sailfish. I doubt if we were more than two miles from the shore the entire time and the weather held up the entire trip. Late afternoon rains were gentle and felt good after the heat of the day on the boats. The conventional fishermen with us had a field day. One 87-year-old angler and his grandson caught and released 116 sailfish in six days of fishing with light tackle!

Cam and I hooked 41 sailfish on flies and lost most to the usual handicaps of fly fishermen. I boated and released 12 sailfish and Cam caught four—an outstanding record for a beginning billfish fly fisherman. My success was aided by a couple of newly-developed Fisher fly rods built by Joe Fisher of Carson City, Nevada. They were proto-type rods of Fisher's Bluewater Fly rod series of rods for big ocean fish. I caught most of my fish on the 3-piece 15-weight Medium rod—which is capable of lifting 22-24 pounds of dead weight—a far cry from the 8-10 pounds most standard 12-13 weight fly rods on the market today are capable of lifting.

Fisher designed the new rods for billfish that dig deep while sounding in the ocean and they are fully capable of bringing fish up from depths without breaking. I put a 20 pound tippet on as terminal tackle for the big 18-weight Heavy model rod and was unable to break it trying to lift fish from the depths.

I brought up a tail-wrapped 100-plus pound sailfish with the heavy rod and anyone who has tried to reel in a tail-wrapped billfish with conventional gear knows what a task that is! Billfish fly rods have finally arrived.

Tropic Star Lodge is approximately a 1-hour flight by twin engine commuter plane south from Panama City. Panama City is an easy jet flight from Miami and such Gulf of Mexico cities as New Orleans and Houston—as well as Dallas/Ft. Worth and Los Angeles.

5

New "Lifting" Fly Rods for Sailfish and Marlin

It is an unfortunate fact that 90 percent of American fly rods that are advertised for sailfish and marlin fishing are not strong enough to lift billfish. Just because a combination graphite and fiberglass fly rod is listed as a 12-14-weight rod does not mean it has the strength to lift a billfish of 100 pounds or more from the depths. It may have excellent fly cast-

ing properties, but that does not mean it is good for sailfish or marlin.

I began considering that problem a few years ago after watching some of my fellow contestants in the first International Billfish Fly Fishing Tournament in Costa Rica fail to lift big sailfish from deep water. I began to think the standard 12-13-weight fly rods being sold for these big fish were too light for the job.

I decided to find out. Using my own (unscientific) testing methods, I tested nine 12-13-weight fly rods. I connected the flyline to a brass Model IN-15 Chatillon scale measuring up to 7 1/2 KG or 15 pounds. Securing the scale to a rigid object, I climbed on a tall ladder and lifted straight up on the fly rods until I felt certain any more pull would break the rods. Since I have broken a total of four 9 foot 12-13-weight graphite fly rods on billfish, I have a certain claim to expertise in this field.

Of all the rods tested—which included three Sage models, a Graphite USA, a Fisher Travel

Facing page: **A custom-made 15-weight, 2-piece big game fly rod made for author Jack Samson, Billy Pate Marlin reel and early double-hooked popper fly designed by the author and marketed by the late Steve Shiba of Edgewater Co.** *Above:* **Bill Barnes fights a big Pacific sailfish on a 12-weight graphite fly rod.**

Rod, an Orvis 9 1/2 foot "tarpon" graphite, a Deerfield 12-weight and an 8 1/2 foot Fenwick 8014 rod, the only fly rod that lifted more than 8 pounds dead weight was the Fenwick. Most of the other rods could only lift between 6-8 pounds. And, theoritically, the Fenwick 8014 would have broken before the 16 pound tippet did—even though it is graded a 14-weight rod!

Now all these fly rods tested are excellent rods. I won the 1989 International Billfish Fly Tournament in Costa Rica with one of Sage's excellent two-piece 13-weight RPL rods and I have used it and others to catch both Atlantic and Pacific sailfish and five species of marlin. I have landed a lot more fish on the current 12-13 weight fly rods than I have broken rods on fish, but are they really strong enough to be called billfish rods? A lot of people in the fly rod designing and building business don't think so.

What really complicated the problem and caused it to surface was the April 1991 decision by the International Game Fish Association to establish a new 20 pound tippet class. If the current fly rods wouldn't lift big fish with 16 pound tippets, what would they do with the 20 pound tippets that became legal April 1991?

Not all rod builders have been unaware of this problem. I fished in Mazatlan with Joe Fisher (who, with his brother, Jim, had developed an excellent line of multiple-piece graphite fly rods) and Joe was trying out both a 15 and 18-weight fly rod on sailfish. Since that time, November 1991, he has come out with both a 2-piece and 3-piece, 8 1/2 foot combination graphite and fiberglass rod that will lift from 20-30 pounds dead weight and still cast well. For years Fisher Rods have built blanks for many other fly rod companies. The secret of success for Fisher has been a combination of the excellent spigot ferrule and the wedge. After a tip or butt graphite pattern has been rolled over its mandrel, a thin wedge-shaped piece of graphite pre-preg is wrapped over each ferrule station with its fibers running around the rod—which reinforces the internal spigots after they are fitted and glued. Fisher's new Bluewater rods for billfish are constructed with oversized guides to permit the easy flow of bulky saltwater knots, an upper cork grip with which lifting power is increased and a special heavy-duty saltwater reel seat.

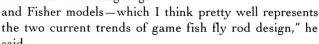

Ian Miller, Australia's best-known rod builder and a light tackle advocate for billfish, approves of the Fisher fly rod.

"I've seen most of the latest blanks—including Sage and Fisher models—which I think pretty well represents the two current trends of game fish fly rod design," he said.

"Personally, I prefer the Fisher style, as the Sage is still a classic casting rod which has been beefed-up to handle extra loading. I don't think it is all that well suited to fighting fish, particularly with the heavier tippets, and do we really need to cast great distances with these rods? I don't think so."

It is becoming increasingly clear to a lot of tarpon and billfish fly rodders that we can't have our rods both ways. Those of us who do a great deal of billfish fly fishing are not interested in the casting qualities of these new rods. In most sailfish and marlin situations, we need only to cast about 20-30 feet behind the boat when fish come up to teaser baits. And since we use 25-30 foot, small-diameter, 12-15 weight-forward sinking shooting heads, it falls into the "chuck-n-duck" school of casting. We pick the big double-hooked billfish flies off the water behind the transom, make one backcast and throw the fly. Accuracy is not a big factor. But when we want to bring that 100-150 pound billfish up from the depths, lifting power is a big factor.

The Fenwick 14-weight 8014 rod has been on the market for some time. Designed by Tim Grennan (who has since left Fenwick), the rod has been the best around for me for a couple of years. Though there have been some rumors that Fenwick plans to reintroduce the old reliable HMG rod, I have not heard that they have any plans to beef-up the 8014. With the new 20 pound tippet, it might not be bad marketing strategy.

In addition to Joe Fisher, there are two other rod designers who are planning for the future of billfish fly fishing in a big way: Steve Rajeff of Loomis and Don Green of Sage. Rajeff, a world class casting champion and expert rod builder, has designed and built some new 8 1/2 foot 13-weight fly rods for Jim and Kelly Watt, the husband and wife team who won the 1991 International Billfish Fly Tournament in Costa Rica—with a total of 10 sailfish.

Not only is Rajeff thinking ahead to the 8 1/2 foot, 2-piece, 13-weight fly rod that will lift 22-23 pounds of dead weight (which his will do now), but he has come up with the same Loomis IMX material 4-piece 14-weight fly rod that will lift between 20-21 pounds of dead weight! This will be a real boon to saltwater billfish and tarpon fly rodders who must travel on planes.

Left: **A beautifully-made 14-weight billfish fly rod by Thomas & Thomas.** *Right:* **The great Medium, 15-weight and Heavy, 18-weight Bluewater 3-piece big game fly rods made by the Fisher Rod Co.—by far the best rods being made today for big sailfish and marlin.**

Not content with planning for the fly rodders who intend to stick with I.G.F.A-approved tippet strength of 16-20 pounds, Loomis is designing rods that will lift as high as 50 pounds dead weight. Rajeff said he has had demands from Australian fly rodders who are fishing for critters like the dog-tooth tuna—running from 50-300 pounds—that dive deep. These anglers are using 30 pound tippets and just want to battle big fish on the long rods.

It is not easy to lift on a fly rod that will pick up 20 pounds of dead weight. If you don't believe me, try it. Rajeff—a powerfully-built man—sticks the butt of these rods in his hip and slowly lifts, with one hand on the cork grip and the other halfway up the bottom section.

"I did this for the Watt's," he said, "and they were just barely able to lift the 20 pound weight off the surface with these rods."

Asked about the decision to stay at the 8 1/2 foot length, Rajeff said he thinks that length is the best compromise between a rod that will still cast well and one that will lift.

Don Green, the master rod designer for Sage Rod Company also feels that the 8 1/2 foot length is the most practical for such big blue water rods—although he is torn between 2-piece and 3-piece rods.

"We are experimenting with the three-piece rod because it takes the center ferrule out of the rod—where the pressure is," he said.

Green, (who was President of Sage Rod when I wrote this book, and has since left the company) was moving in a direction which is very interesting to me as a billfish fly fisherman. Although Sage can build both 2-piece and 3-piece fly rods that will lift up to 30 and 40 pounds, Don had a theory that the rod should be built to lift just under the tippet strength weight. At the moment he had built prototype rods that will lift just under the 16 pound tippet dead weight. Now that the 20 pound tippet class has been introduced, he was designing a rod that will lift a dead weight of just about 18-19 pounds—for that new tippet category.

He agreed with my theory that if you fasten a 16 pound leader to a fence post and try to break that tippet with a steady pull of any current 12-13 weight fly rod, the rod would break first.

"Yes," he said, "But if you do the same thing with a fly rod that can lift 17 pounds dead weight, you are going to break the tippet first. In designing rods, my theory has been that if you are using 8 kilo shock tippets (16 pound), you really don't want a rod that will lift a great deal more than that—or you are just going to pop the leader."

What we may well wind up with in the not too distant future is fly rods for big ocean fish being stamped with

something like DW-16 or DW-20 to designate the dead weight lifting capability of the rod—in addition to its designation of rod weight. This would be for fly rodders who intend to fish for billfish under the current regulations set forth by the I.G.F.A. It would not apply to anglers who just want to catch big billfish on a fly rod—regardless of tippet strength. For example, excellent saltwater fly rodder, Mike Sakamoto of Hawaii, was the first man to catch a Pacific blue marlin on a fly. He used Fenwick's 8014 rod and trolled a big popper behind a boat—using a leader far in excess of I.G.F.A rules. He wasn't interested in setting world records. He just wanted to catch a blue marlin—which he certainly did. The fish weighed an incredible 206 pounds.

As is true of any industry, there are probably all sorts of internal secrets. I am sure there are any number of other rod builders who are interested in this new family of saltwater fly rods for big fish, but who have not talked about their research. All this should come out in the next few years—as interest mushrooms in better fly rods for sailfish and marlin—spurned on by the I.G.F.A starting the new 20 pound tippet category.

A group of the best early "big game" fly rods available in about 1990. The strongest was the Fenwick 8014.

CHAPTER

6

Large Sailfish of Costa Rica

The big sailfish came up to the trolled, hookless strip bait as we were fishing long Pacific swells in

the sleek, 31-foot Rampage, the *Amie Marie*, about 20 miles out of Garza Bay on the west coast of

Costa Rica.

"Sail!" shouted Bob, the mate, from the tower and Don Tompkins, the boat owner, scrambled to

get the big squids in from the starboard outrigger while I

grabbed the long teaser rod from the gunwale holder.

To my right, Billy Pate picked up his 12-weight fly rod and

stood ready as the sailfish repeatedly slashed at the skipping

dorado belly I was rapidly reeling in.

"Get ready, Billy," I said as the bait skidded to within 40

feet of the transom—the hungry sail right behind it.

"Let him eat it, Jack," Billy said, picking up his rod tip and

holding the white double-hooked streamer fly with his left hand, "Then yank it away."

I let the strip bait drop back and sink and the sailfish immediately grabbed it. I let the sailfish

take hold then pointed the rod tip at the fish and jerked the bait from the fish's mouth. It sailed off

to my left as I felt Bob drop the boat into neutral. Pate's fly landed about 5 feet to the far side of the

sailfish and as he stripped the fly rapidly on the surface, the sailfish turned and took the fly.

Above: **Author Samson fights a big fly-hooked sailfish off the fine big game resort of Bahia Pez Vela on the west coast of Costa Rica.** *Facing page:* **A happy mate holds a big Pacific sailfish just caught by Billy Pate.**

As Pate struck hard several times, the sailfish took to the air in a series of skittering leaps.

"Good fish!" Don shouted as Bob eased the throttles of the twin-diesels forward—helping to keep slack out of the shooting head, running line and 30 pound backing on the big fly reel. Billy had the 9 foot graphite rod held high as the sailfish continued to jump 150 yards out from the boat.

I stowed the teaser rod and bait as Don brought in all the teaser squids and a couple of big teasers on a flat line close to the transom.

"OK to start backing down," Billy shouted up to Bob as the sailfish finished jumping and settled down to an underwater fight. I looked at my watch. It was 3:35 p.m. on a beautiful afternoon in early April. There was a slight haze on the water and it cast a film over the surrounding sea.

Bob maneuvered the Sportfisherman easily in the moderate sea as Billy began to pump the sail in rhythmically. It was not more than 10 minutes before most of the 100 feet of 30 pound monofilament running line was back on the reel and I could see the 30 feet of 12-weight forward fast-sinking shooting head in the clear water.

"Fly line coming up," I said to Don and the big Maine-raised man slipped on a pair of gloves with which to hold the fish's bill.

Pate leaned back and lifted the sailfish from the depths with the big fly rod as Bob eased back on the throttles. I got a camera from the forward cabin as Don leaned down and grasped the sailfish by the bill—sliding it gently over the edge of the transom. Both men held the fish's sail spread as I took several photographs.

"Beautiful fish," said Bob leaning over the edge of the tower, "What'll it weigh?"

"'Bout a hundred pounds, wouldn't you say, Jack?"

Don said. I nodded and looked at my watch again. It was 3:51—about a normal amount of time for Pate to subdue a sailfish on a fly rod. Don gently lowered the tired billfish over the side—where we watched it swim slowly away in the royal blue of the ocean.

"Nice job on the teaser rod," Billy said to me as we shook hands. "Get your fly rod. It's your turn."

It was our third day fishing with Don and his Bahia Garza Fishing Charters and the fishing had been a bit slow—probably because of the stage of the moon. It was only a week past full moon. But we had a number of hookups on sailfish and had seen a few blue marlin come up to inspect the baits. We were to leave early the following morning to fish Quepos—about 150 miles to the south. While Don and his wife, Kim, run a fine fishing operation out of Garza Bay, the surf was very high and there was no shelter in the bay for berthing boats. The two new Rampages had to be moored about 100 yards from shore and getting to and from them in the morning and evening was more of an adventure than Pate and I wanted to continue. We had capsized twice—once in a rubber raft and once in a leaky row boat—trying to get through the giant combers rolling in from the Pacific. Both Pate and I are good swimmers, but we carried a small fortune in rods, reels and camera gear and we had decided we would rather not risk them any more.

Don Tompkins agreed that the surf was a bit much at Garza and was taking his two boats up to Flamingo Beach—about 85 miles to the north—where he charters them for the late spring, summer and fall.

The following day we flew down to Quepos in the early morning—arriving about 9 a.m.—where we were met by Bill Gannon, veteran skipper of one of the four 27 foot center-console Strike boats of Sportfishing Costa Rica. The Strike boats are sleek, fast sportfishermen that get anglers out to sailfish and marlin waters in approximately 30 minutes from the sheltered harbor of Quepos. A secure harbor is one of the biggest problems for fishermen on the west coast of Costa Rica.

Quepos has a deep, sheltered harbor that has been used for years by big commercial vessels and fishing boats alike. It has a huge commercial dock and plenty of mooring space for small boats. The dock area lies against a bluff just south of the small town of Quepos itself—a small, pleasantly sleepy tropical town with hundreds of private homes, small inns, hotels and restaurants perched in the hills above.

We were on the fishing grounds in a 30 minute run out from the snug harbor. The blue water—in an approximately 4-knot current that runs north along the spectacularly rugged coast—swings in close to land at this spot. Quepos

Above: **Pate measures the sailfish prior to release. The formula is: measure the girth and square that number. Then measure the length—from the tip of the lower bill to the fork of the tail—and multiply those two numbers. Then divide the result by 800 for the weight.** *Facing page top:* **A big fly-hooked sailfish tail-walks off Costa Rica.** *Middle:* **A spent sailfish comes alongside.** *Bottom:* **Author and happy crew of the *Cubero* bring aboard a 105 pound Pacific sailfish off Bahia Pez Vela, Costa Rica.**

has good fishing for billfish, tuna, dorado, big snapper and grouper, wahoo, amberjack and roosterfish year-round.

The first day out we hooked up with four sailfish and saw two blue marlin—one small enough to be a quarry for a fly rodder. The weather off Quepos is calm most of the time because of the geographical location. While the wind howls in gale-force strength from December to April on the northern coast of Costa Rica, Quepos is separated from the strong winds by a mountain range that runs roughly east and west.

Billy Pate fished the Quepos area for two weeks the following February—while making a new video on catching sailfish with a fly—and saw 180 billfish that investigated the trolled baits. He cast to 120 fish and hooked and released 50 sailfish in that period—no mean feat for a fly fisherman.

In the three days we fished there in April we raised about 20 sailfish and hooked up with about 12 fish. We had one very good follow from a small blue marlin and might have hooked up with it, but the 30 pound mono teaser line broke when the fish took the bait. It broke again on a sailfish about an hour later as Pate handled the teaser rod—leaving us to believe the line was defective. We changed it and rigged up with much stronger line on the teaser rod—50 pound mono.

There are quite a few blue marlin in the area and we had another hungry marlin come up and take the plastic squid off a daisy chain of squid trolled on a flat line just behind the transom!

But the weather remained fine and the sailfish surfaced behind the baits, took flies well and danced their aerial ballet on the surface of the sea in a land made for fishermen—especially fly fishermen who try for billfish on the long rods.

7
Terminal Tackle For Big Fish

There are so many variations in terminal fly tackle for big ocean fish it is no wonder the novice becomes discouraged. I average about four or five long-distance phone calls a week from young beginning saltwater fly rodders who are hoping to try for big blue water fish and the conversation usually starts out like this:

"Look, I've been trying to find out what kind of knots to tie for the fly, the shock leader, the class tippet, the running line and the backing, and I must have called a dozen fly shops, two reel companies and a couple of rod companies that make big ocean rods and either they don't know or they all give me a different answer!"

It is understandable. The sport of fly fishing for big ocean fish is so new that hardly anyone has figured out a fool-proof system yet for terminal tackle. There is even considerable disagreement about knots and materials among those of us who fish for such fish as sailfish, marlin, sharks, tuna and dorado on a regular basis. But those differences of opinion are fairly minor—which size hook is best, which knot is stronger, etc.

I have come up with what I think is the simplest and the strongest big game terminal rig there is. It is easy to make, the connections are all 100 percent in strength and it conforms to I.G.F.A rules for fly fishing. For want of any more imaginative name I call it the Samson Rig—strength guarenteed.

When I first began fly fishing for big fish in the late 1960s there were not many people doing it. Billy Pate, Stu Apte, Lee Wulff, Lee Cuddy and Dr. Webster Robinson were about the only people in the world who had caught a

sailfish or marlin on a fly. Everybody was experimenting—with rods, reels, backing, lines, leaders and flies. Most of us started out with weight-forward floating fly lines—which proved to be too long and too bulky to travel through the water at high speeds. The large diameter of the floating lines had too much resistance to

Facing page: **The strongest connections in the terminal tackle for billfish can be achieved by using metal connector sleeves that are squeezed tight with crimping pliers.** *Above:* **A fly hangs up in the bill of a Pacific sailfish off Mazatlan.**

the water when billfish greyhounded across the ocean surface at speeds between 50-60 mph.

The lines didn't break, but the tippets did and the maximum tippet strength then was 16 pounds. The ultimate answer was to go to short, (25-30 foot) small-diameter, heavy shooting heads, but that left us with the small-diameter 30 pound backing connecting to the short shooting head. The trouble with that was the backing cut through the skin of the hand or fingers while setting a hook in a big fish.

Pate soon came up with answers to that problem by going to lengths of mono running line (30-40 pound test) between the backing and the fly line.

The same problem existed for anglers fly fishing for big tarpon with shooting heads—although tarpon, while they jump a lot, don't travel at the sizzling speeds billfish do.

As we added more sections of line, leader and backing, knots became more and more important. The knots that connected the fly to the heavy 12 inch shock leader (80-100 pound in tarpon and billfish), the shock leader to the class tippet, the knot in the class tippet double line, the class tippet to the butt leader section, the butt leader to the fly line, the fly line to the running line, and the running line to the backing, became a vital factor in terminal tackle.

I venture to guess that more fish were lost to poorly tied (or the wrong) knots than anything else in big game tackle.

I started out using a 3 1/2 turn clinch knot to connect my fly to the 100 pound shock leader. Though I caught a lot of tarpon that way I lost a lot of sailfish when the knot slipped. I used an Albright knot to fasten the class tippet to the shock leader and have never had that knot slip there. But I have had the Albright knot pull out in the connection between the backing and running line and lost a nice marlin at Cabo San Lucas in the summer of 1991 for that reason.

I began using the nail knot to fasten the 3 foot butt leader section to the fly line, but have had that knot pull out several times on big fish. Billy Pate swears by a double (or back-to-back) nail knot between the fly line and butt section and between fly line and running line, but I find it too bulky when running through the rod guides. Bulky knots have cost me several big fish. I lost a big striped marlin a few years back off Mazatlan after trying to fasten 40 pound mono running line to the backing with a loop-to-loop connection. The line—whistling off the reel while the marlin jumped—hung up on that knot and the tippet parted.

I use a spider hitch or five-times-around knot to form the double line knot in the class tippet and have never had that knot break. It is a strong knot, far easier to tie than the complicated Bimini twist and every bit as strong in mono of less than 30 pound strength. The Bimini gained popularity with anglers using conventional gear and lines from 30-130 pound test. The double line section of the class tippet has been formed for years and why we make a double line is beyond me—although it certainly can do no harm.

There is no stronger knot connection than the double surgeon's loop used loop-to-loop between sections of mono and mono to 30 pound Micron or Dacron backing—or for that matter between fly line and butt leader or fly line and running line. But, thanks to the Berkley (or Jinkai) connector sleeve, there is now a simpler way to connect fly line, backing and mono.

Let me use a 20 pound tippet section of mono as an example. I take a 5 foot section of the 20 pound mono and form a double line of several feet in length at one end—using a spider hitch. Then, making sure the single strand is at least 15 inches long (I.G.F.A rules) I fasten the class tippet to the 12 inch 100 pound length of shock leader with an Albright knot. This knot is about the best I know for connecting mono of vastly different diameters and I have never had this knot pull out or break in mono.

The knot that connects the 100 pound shock leader to the fly should allow the fly to swing free—helping its action and making it easier to set at angles. For that pur-

Above: **The best way to fasten a billfish fly to 100 pound shock leader: Pass mono through hook eye then through a .098, #5 Berkley sleeve. Squeeze down with a pair of crimping pliers then trim tag end—leaving fly to swing free.** *Facing page top:* **The excellent big game reel, the Fin-Nor #5 anti-reverse model. Note foam head, with eyes, slid down the leader in front of the fly.** *Left:* **The best fly line for billfish: A 30-foot, high density, 518-grain, fast-sinking, narrow and heavy shooting head—which has a breaking strength of about 45 pounds.** *Right:* **A .098, #5 Berkley connector sleeve makes the strongest connection between the fly line and the loop end of the butt leader.**

pose I slip a #5 Berkley connector sleeve (nickel-plated size .098) over the end of the shock leader, pass it through the hook eye to form a loop then squeeze it down tight with a pair of crimping pliers.

I then connect the class tippet double line to the fly line using two double surgeon's knot loops—loop-to-loop. I make a loop in the end of the fly line and secure it with a similiar connector sleeve.

I then form the same loop in the other end of the fly line with a connector sleeve and loop-to-loop that one to a loop at the end of a 100 foot section of 45 pound soft mono. The loop at the end of the running line is formed by using a smaller connector sleeve—a #3 (size .062). The same small sleeve can form a similar loop at the other end of the running line and that can be connected to the 30 pound backing by a double surgeon's loop.

That system gives an almost fool-proof terminal rig that may not be pretty (if one is a knot fancier) but is strong. The small connector sleeves pass easily through the rod guides and don't have to pass through very often anyway as they are at the end of the line. If one is concerned the metal sleeves might nick guides, coat them with Pliobond or clear nail polish.

The choice of leader, line and backing is up to the individual, but I have found the best for my purposes is Mason mono for the class tippet. It is a very hard mono and resists abrasion and nicks. The brand of 100 pound shock leader doesn't matter much. I have settled upon 30 feet of Cortland's 444, Type 6, ST 15S shooting head fly line. It has a very small diameter, is quite heavy (518 grains), strong and easy to cast.

Any 40-45 pound test mono will work well for running line, but I use a 45 pound test mono named Schneider. I learned about it from Billy Pate, it is soft and very stretchable. This line is made in West Germany and is difficult to find. I get mine from Jack Erskine who is an excellent saltwater fly fisherman who operates a tackle shop in Cairns, Australia. I have used 30 pound Micron as backing for years, but recently have switched to 36 pound Cortland Green Spot.

8

Atlantic Blue Marlin on a Fly

The green-colored shallow water close to the beach suddenly changes color to a royal blue not 100 yards offshore. The only place I know where that happens is the famous drop-off at Havana, Cuba— where I fished the first Hemingway Invitational Billfish Tournament in 1978.

"My God!" I said, looking at Wes Ruggles, captain of the 23 foot Seacraft *El Picante*. "Where did the bottom go?"

"This is The Wall," he laughed. "It goes half way to Japan for all I know. How do you want to rig up?" he asked "I'm new to this fly fishing for billfish. You want the outriggers?"

"Just the starboard one," I said. "I need to make a back cast from the port corner of the cockpit and that 'rigger would be in the way. We can run a Kona head on the starboard 'rigger and stick the other boat rod up in the tower with you. The mate can bring in the starboard lure and you can crank in the top one—the

balao with no hook in it. Just keep it ahead of the fish until you get it in pretty close and then yank it away from him. I'll get a fly to him while you slip the motor into neutral."

"Got it," Wes said waving to the young, blond mate, Butch Buie, to let the outrigger down.

I ran a daisy chain of tan plastic squids back about 20 feet behind the transom as a teaser and fastened it to the starboard cleat. We could leave the squid there if the billfish came up. I rigged Wes's boat rod with a hookless balao from the bait well and tossed it into the wake. He ran it back about 60 feet—about even with the yellow and green strip-festooned Kona head Butch ran back from the starboard outrigger. Wes

Above: **Balao fly, tied by the author, caught the Atlantic blue marlin off the east coast of Mexico.** *Facing page:* **Author Samson brings the Atlantic blue marlin alongside the *Picante* after an hour-long battle.**

adjusted the throttle of the 235-hp outboard and the trim, little boat settled into trolling speed. There was a fair chop and the wind blew steadily from the northeast. I stripped off the 30 feet of sinking shooting head, 20 pound class tippet, 100 pound shock and fly and coiled them on the deck in the port corner of the cockpit. I leaned the 15-weight fly rod against the transom and settled down to watch the trolled bait and lures.

The trip was a last-minute affair. A television crew from Phoenix, Arizona had called me the week before and asked if I'd be interested in trying to catch a sailfish for a video on billfish on a fly. I will go anywhere to fish for sails and marlin with a fly rod, but had warned them it might not be as easy as it sounded. One didn't just "cue up" a billfish on demand—especially when using a fly. But they were enthusiastic and insisted we try.

They were considerably less enthusiastic this morning—after being buffeted by a rough sea all the day before—waiting in vain for a billfish to surface behind our larger charter boat. When I showed up ready to try again, the producer/director told me the television crew had decided to go out with several anglers using conventional gear and 30 pound line. They wanted footage of billfish being hooked and fought, said the young producer, and they figured the chances were a lot better with standard tackle.

"Maybe we can try it again with you in a couple of days," he said. "After these guys get enough footage in the can to make up a show."

I nodded—wondering what to do with the rest of the day.

I was contemplating a day on the beach when a pleasant-looking fellow in shorts and a white T-shirt walked up.

"Excuse me," he said, "but I couldn't help overhearing that conversation. You're a fly fisherman, right?"

I nodded and we shook hands.

"Listen," he said, "I've got a small boat, but she's seaworthy and I'd be happy if you'd try her out, I've never seen billfish caught on a fly, but I sure would like to."

It took about 20 minutes for us to organize that fishing trip and head out through the marina—as a bright, May sun beat down on the cobalt blue sea.

The huge, new, opulent Oasis Hotel—located about 60 miles south of the resort city of Cancun on Mexico's Yucatan coast couldn't have been placed in a better spot for big game fishermen. The fabulous drop-off runs for miles along the coast and one can see the tall buildings on the island of Cozumel, famous for its billfish—about 15 miles away. As a matter of fact the boats from Cozumel come over to the coast each morning in the spring for sailfish and marlin. Sails, white and Atlantic blue marlin are plentiful along the palm-studded coast during the peak of the season—March, April and May.

"Billfish!" Butch suddenly shouted, leaping to bring in the Kona head. I saw the bill slash rapidly at the lure as the mate quickly reeled in. Then, as I reached for the fly rod, I saw the billfish switch its attack to the trolled balao and quickly engulf it before Wes could reel it in.

The skipper tried to take the teaser bait away from the fish, but it was too late. A sailfish of about 40 pounds suddenly began tailwalking away from us while Wes fought to regain the bait. As Butch and I cheered him on, Wes fought the sail until it disgorged the bait about 100 yards from the boat. I held it up when Wes got it back. It had been shredded by the hungry sailfish.

A number of bigger boats around us were fighting sailfish and Wes stayed in touch with them on the radio. The anglers with the video camera crew had not seen any billfish, he reported, and couldn't help smiling.

"Pretty good action for this late in May," he said as we began to troll again. "It's been pretty quiet the last few days. I think the billfish are moving north and we are about through with the season—although there will be plenty of big blues and tuna in the channel between here and Cozumel the rest of the summer and fall."

The bill came up behind the teaser bait an hour later. Wes saw it and grabbed for the rod holding the balao. He reeled frantically as the fish continued to slash at the bait. The speeding fish was already well within casting distance.

"Neutral, Wes," I shouted and made a back cast. The balao imitation fly landed close to the searching fish as the boat slowed. I made one quick strip of the fly and the billfish lunged from the water and took the fly. Butch skidded in the Kona head lure and reached for the line holding the squid daisy chain.

The billfish climbed out of the water behind us and went greyhounding off across the ocean surface.

"Marlin!" Wes shouted as the fish took out several hundred yards of 30 pound backing. "I can't tell if it's a white or a blue—jumping that way into the sun."

"It's a small blue, I think," Butch said hauling in the squid teaser. "The dorsal fin is pointed. The white's dorsal is rounded."

The marlin finally stopped jumping about 300 yards out and Wes began backing the boat into the sea. The water came over the low transom as the outboard's prop bit into the water.

That little blue marlin was a tough fish and put up a stubborn battle in the depths before finally giving up about 50 minutes later. I brought it alongside and Butch grabbed the bill. The double-hooked fly was lodged in the corner of its mouth. Wes leaned over the rail of the tower and took several photographs as Butch removed the fly and we released the brilliantly-striped marlin to grow bigger. Wes estimated its weight at about 65 pounds.

"That's the first Atlantic blue marlin caught here on a fly that I know about," Wes said. "A couple of

whites and a number of sails have been caught over at Cozumel, but I haven't heard of any blues caught on a fly. It's a first for the *El Picante*—that's for sure!"

It was my second Atlantic blue marlin on a fly. I caught a small one on a fly off Jamaica in 1983, but this was the first one of mine photographed being boated and released.

The producer/director of the video show was very upset when he heard the little blue marlin jumped 17 times after being hooked. Nobody has ever gotten video shots of a fly-hooked Atlantic blue marlin being fought and landed. His crew could have been the first—with a little more patience.

"That sure was too bad about missing all that action," Wes said, watching the producer/director walk away across the hotel lobby. Then he looked at me and winked.

"Just think," he added thoughtfully. "You just missed being a movie star."

Facing page: **Capt. Wesley Ruggles' trim 23-foot Seacraft** *El Picante* - "the hot one"- with a 235-hp Johnson outboard motor—the ideal big game boat for the fly fisherman. *Above:* **Mate Butch Buie grabs the bill and the author the tail. The smiles of both speak a million words.**

9
Flies for Billfish

A good many years ago in the Florida Keys it was thought that all one needed to catch billfish on a fly was a piece of cork with some tail feathers stuck in it. As a matter of fact that was what the first man to catch a sailfish on a fly, Webster "Doc" Robinson of Florida, used to take his first billfish on a fly—a 74 1/2 pound sail off the Florida Keys. Doc's prototype lure—certainly by today's standards—was a fairly primitive creation. It was a white-painted, flat-bottomed cork popper with a couple of white feathers inserted in the rear.

Like a lot of us who later were to take up the sport of billfish on a fly, Doc believed the surface commotion of a popper was the key to strikes. Billy Pate carved a white cork popper in the early 1970s that

worked well on billfish—though he preferred to use the double-hooked, white side hackle streamer fly for which he is credited.

In California the late, great saltwater fly fisherman Harry Kime, was experimenting with large flies off the east coast of Baja in the 1960s in an effort to catch billfish. Although he caught a number of sailfish with his highly-successful "Tutie-

Top: **Billy Pate's original double-hooked, white saddle hackle billfish fly—with which he caught all his world record sailfish and marlin.** *Bottom:* **Double-hooked billfish poppers.** *Facing page:* **A collection of Cam Sigler's colorful billfish tube flies. They are double-hooked and interchangeable—to alternate colors and combinations.**

Top left: **One of Don Drown's colorful double-hooked billfish poppers.** *Top right:* **Drown's effective double-hooked billfish streamers—mounted on 8/0 stainless steel hooks for marlin.** *Bottom left:* **Author Samson's double-hooked (7/0 Mustad 34007) blue Bonito fly.** *Bottom right:* **Samson's double-hooked green mackerel fly—used for billfish off Cabo San Lucas during green mackerel months.** *Below:* **Author's Balao fly on 7/0 hooks.** *Facing page:* **A display of author's double-hooked billfish flies tied on 7/0 hooks. Bottom fly is the highly-successful dorado imitation.**

Frutie" foam-bodied fly, he was never able to land a marlin with it. The fly had a square foam body with a handful of chicken feathers inserted into the rear. Harry colored the entire body and dyed the feathers orange—painting on spots with a marking pencil. Harry believed in large hooks for billfish and mounted his creation on both 7/0 and 8/0 stainless steel Mustad hooks.

The orange color also held a fascination for pioneer billfish fly fisherman Winston Moore—who has caught more than 100 sailfish in his long career. He first experimented with a white-painted, flat-bottom cork popper with a

white-feathered tail, like Doc Robinson, but finally gave it up in favor of streamer flies with a popper head. Moore's use of a soft head in front of a streamer is probably the first time it was done—back in the early 1970s. As to Moore being the first billfish fly rodder to use the sliding popper head:

"I experimented with Styrofoam and all kinds of materials," he wrote, "and finally settled on this particular soft foam as it is bouyant enough to float, but absorbent enough to take on a little water which keeps it from bouncing all over when the fish strikes. I believe I was the originator of the sliding popper head; at least in those days no one I knew had even thought of it."

Billy Pate obviously never felt any improvement was necessary for his white side hackle billfish streamer—at least as far as color was concerned. He has, however, in the last decade added foam popper heads to his shock leaders to act as an attractor. The late Lee Wulff, a pioneer saltwater fly fisherman, tied his own big flies for billfish and sort of made a compromise between the standard fly and a close imitation of baitfish. His double-hooked flies with barred feathers and bright green and yellow colors, closely resembled small bait-

fish than the earlier, simpler patterns, the more sophisticated flies certainly catch billfish regularly.

One of the first fly tiers to come up with a lifelike billfish fly was Joe Butorac of Washington state. His excellent blue and white double-hooked balao fly definitely appeals to sailfish and marlin. With it Jim and Kelly Watt won the 1990 International Billfish Fly Tournament in Costa Rica with 10 sailfish. Most catalogs today carry his fly as the one for billfish—accompanied by a white and blue foam popper head.

I had the same experience with poppers that Winston Moore did. In the mid-1970s I began experimenting with cork poppers—modeled after Billy Pate's single-hook white version. I added a trailing hook of a 3/0 Mustad 34007 hook, but I missed more sailfish than I hooked. Even though I was a co-winner of the 1989 International Billfish Fly Tournament at Flamingo Bay, Costa Rica—using my home-made, double-hooked cork popper—I was not satisfied with the lure. The late Steve Shiba of Edgewater Flies worked with me for a couple of years designing a porous-type body for my popper and—even though it is marketed today—I am convinced the body should be of a much softer material. Billfish first slash at a fly with their bill then turn and engulf it. If the body is hard the billfish clamps down on it and holds on while the angler tries to set the hook in a soft part of the mouth. Then—when the fish opens its mouth and releases the lure—the fly comes out without the hooks catching in anything.

The trend to a soft, foam popper just ahead of a double-hooked streamer fly makes a lot of sense. When a fish closes its mouth the popper head is squeezed down and the hooks are more likely to sink in when the angler strikes. Cam Sigler, an excellent freshwater fly fisherman and one who also has considerable experience catching billfish on a fly, has come up with his own tube flies for sailfish and marlin. They have the advantage of being easy to connect and one can put together variations of the same fly in minutes.

fish—complete with a brightly painted yellow and black eye. This fly was the one Wulff reputedly used to catch his 148 pound striped marlin off Salinas, Ecuador in 1967—still a record on 12 pound tippet today.

But there is another school of billfish fly anglers that advocates a more "match-the-hatch" approach to fly fishing for sailfish and marlin—along the lines of freshwater fly fishing expert Ernie Schweibert's system of fly fishing for trout. Schweibert contended that tying trout flies to match aquatic insects as closely as possible improved one's chances of taking these wily game fish.

A good many billfish fly anglers have begun to use larger double-hooked streamer flies—with an accompanying soft foam popper head—that make an attempt to closely imitate the natural baitfish upon which billfish feed. While there is no accurate way to tell if these flies take more bill-

Top left: **Beautifully-made billfish streamer fly (Don Drown).** *Middle left:* **Author-tied blue mullet billfish fly alongside Sage's excellent 13-weight big game fly rod.** *Right:* **Effective squid billfish fly tied by veteran saltwater fly rodder Terry Baird.**

I began to tie my own imitations of baitfish a few years ago and now use nothing else. I had grown weary of billfish coming up for the teasers and turning away from or completely ignoring the standard flies I was using. I tied double-hooked flies to imitate the most common prey of billfish: dorado, flying fish, bonito, balao, mullet and mackerel. They are carried today by that excellent commercial fly tier, Otto Beck of Pittsburg, Pennsylvania.

By 1991 Don Drown had come up with some spectacular large double-hooked billfish flies tied on 7/0 and 8/0 hooks. The only catalog I know that carries such flies is the TAG Offshore Tackle from Edgartown, Massachusetts.

Most of the catalogs that carry both fresh and saltwater flies seem to completely ignore the large billfish fly field — all except TAG, World Wide and International Angler — which carries an excellent sailfish fly designed by Winston Moore. Big order houses like Kaufmann's Streamborn and Orvis — long a pioneer in fly fishing — seem to have missed the boat when it comes to billfish flies.

Sophisticated, well-designed billfish flies that accurately imitate baitfish are not easy to tie up nor are they inexpensive. Most sell from $18-$25 because a lot of very expensive material goes into them — and they take considerable time to construct. But, believe me, by the time you add up air fare, hotel room, the cost of a day's boat charter, drinks and food, the cost of a good billfish fly is the least expensive item of the trip. Besides, one doesn't get many shots at billfish with a fly and they hold up well. I have seen as many as five Pacific sailfish caught on a fly before it became too battered to use any more.

Top: **Billfish mullet flies as tied by Terry Baird.** *Bottom:* **Joe Butorac's very successful double-hooked billfish fly.**

10

Fly Rod-Size Black Marlin

For the fly rodder, marlin are never a sure thing but the small, acrobatic black marlin of Australia's northern Queensland coast are as close to it as one can get.

From August to November each year small black marlin—in the 25 to 100 pound range—can be found in impressive numbers from the area of Cape Bowling Green south of Townsville up to the storied fishing port of Cairns.

Billy Pate, the legendary fly fisherman from Islamorada, Florida—who caught the very first black marlin on a fly off Cairns in 1972—told me about the spot a few years back. At the time it didn't mean much to me as I had no particular reason to travel that far in search of billfish.

Going to Australia to try for a black was way down on my list of priorities. Then I received an invitation from Warren Allen of Aussie Game Fishing Agencies in Townsville, Australia, to come down and try for a small black aboard the 40 foot Sportfisherman, *Seaducer*, skippered by veteran Captain Calvin Tilley. Calvin was the first man to discover and develop the marvelous fishing for black marlin and sailfish in the Cape Bowling Green area and wanted me to take a look.

Pathways International of Newbury, New Hampshire—specializing in outfitting sportsmen for trips to Australia and New Zealand—quickly organized the trip. American Airlines had a quick, comfortable round-trip flight that left for Sydney, Australia from Dallas/Ft. Worth three times a week via Honolulu. One left

---

Facing page: **Ian Miller reaches for the bill of a small black marlin.** *Above:* **Author watches line stream from reel as black marlin jumps far from boat.**

at 6:40 p.m. and arrived in Sydney at 5:00 a.m. the following morning (skipping a day at the International Date Line). Australian Airlines gets one from Sydney to Townsville before noon. You can be fishing the same day.

The black marlin grounds are approximately a 1 1/2 to 2 hour run from Townsville—south to a spot about 10 miles northwest of Cape Bowling Green. Captain Tilley utilizes a posh 75 foot, luxury mother

ship, the *Pacific Adventure*, from which to fish each day. The mother ship is anchored in the calm lee of the Cape and the *Seaducer* ties up to her each night—making the 20 minute run to the marlin grounds each morning. Those not wishing to stay on a mother ship have a two hour run to and from the grounds to Townsville—though hotel accommodations in Townsville are excellent.

Calvin Tilley invited rod builder Ian Miller and outdoor writer Steve Starling along to fish and—though neither was a fly fisherman—both were veteran marlin anglers. The first day saw several small blacks caught by the two on live bait and one marlin took a big 5/0 double-hooked deer hair streamer fly tied for me by Tom Nokes, of Troutsmen Enterprises in Sandy, Utah. After about six exciting jumps the hook pulled out and the marlin got away, but it was enough to convince me it was possible for me to catch a black on a fly.

After switching to a smaller fly—a blue and white streamer with 4/0 double hooks, tied by Joe Butorac of Washington state—we went out again on Sunday, August 12th to try again. Shortly before noon a black came up and slashed at the hookless port balao teaser bait.

"Billfish!" shouted Captain Tilley and mate Alan Zavodny scrambled to bring in the teaser. Ian Miller hurriedly brought in the hookless starboard teaser and some Kona heads skipping off the starboard outrigger.

In the port corner of the cockpit, I quickly let the fly run back about 20 feet in the wake—ready for a back cast. When Alan jerked the teaser from the water, I shouted 'O.K.!' and picked the fly off the water. Captain Tilley slipped the controls into neutral. The blue and white fly landed about 6 feet to the left of the searching marlin and, with a quick surge, it took the fly—streaking to my left and coming half out of water.

I dropped the rod to my right and set the hook several times with a series of hard jerks. The marlin took off across the surface of the sea—greyhounding to the east

and throwing spray on each jump in the bright morning sunlight. I raised the rod tip high and let the big Pate reel absorb all the punishment as the marlin peeled off the 30 feet of fast-sinking shooting head, the 100 feet of 40 pound test monofilament running line and 30 pound Micron backing. At about 200 yards out, the black dove and sounded for the depths.

The *Seaducer* began backing down in a following sea and the line began to slant upward toward the surface. The marlin came out again and began another series of thrashing jumps—ending with a spectacular cartwheel jump that threw water in all directions as the fish fell back to the surface.

At 45 minutes, I had the little marlin coming in and was putting all the pressure I dared on the 9 foot, 12-weight graphite fly rod. The fish was directly below the stern and I was leaning backward—the rod bent double—when the rod snapped at the big ferrule with a deafening crack. With a sickening feeling, I held the butt of the rod and bottom section away from the transom, hoping to keep the fish on. The leader held, however, and the mate leaned far over the gunwale and jabbed a yellow, plastic release tag into the shoulder of the struggling marlin.

"O.K. mate," he said grinning, "He's all yours now—no matter what happens."

The black—tired now—came up slowly as I tried to lift it with the shattered rod. Too close to the stern, it dove into the spinning port propeller and nicked its bill before careening to the surface. The mate reached out with a gaff and hooked it around the bill—drawing the marlin close to the stern where he grasped it by the bill and hauled it aboard.

There were shouts, back-slapping and much hand-shaking as the mate held the little black aloft—his arms wrapped around the struggling fish. We took the fish's measurements and estimated the weight at 50 pounds—before photographing it and releasing it to grow into one of the 1,000-plus pound monsters the Australians refer to as "granders." I caught one of those huge 1,000 pound black marlins in 1980 on 80 pound line at Lizard Island, north of Cairns, and believe me I enjoyed the fight with the little black on a fly rod a whole lot more!

We fished the rest of that day and another before I quit and returned to the States—exhausted by jet-lag but triumphant at catching the black on a fly.

Above: **Captain Calvin Tilly watches outrigger lures.** *Facing page top:* **The mother ship *Pacific Adventure* rests at anchor behind the Great Barrier Reef off Townsville, Australia.** *Bottom:* **Mate Allan Zavodny and author Samson inspect small Pacific black marlin before release.**

CHAPTER

11

Teasing and Hooking Billfish on a Fly

While there is no doubt the biggest thrill in fighting billfish on a fly is the acrobatics, one has to get the sailfish or marlin close to the boat and interested in a fly first. Perhaps the most difficult part of fly fishing for billfish is setting the hook in the tough cartilage of the mouth. The long whippy fly rod is not the best tool for driving the barb of a hook home.

I.G.F.A rules—for world record fish only—stipulate that the boat must be out of gear when the fly is cast to the fish. This is an unnecessary rule as anyone who has caught sailfish and marlin on a fly knows it is extremely difficult to hook a billfish unless the boat *is* either out of gear or nearly stopped. While a boat is moving the billfish is following the lures or teaser and it is almost impossible to set a hook in the bill of a sailfish or marlin. The bill is composed of a tough, thorny material—as hard as bone—and even though a very sharp hook might sometimes "hang up" on the bill, the first few jumps usually flip it free. It is necessary to have the boat out of gear, or almost stopped, so that the billfish may either take the fly from an angle or turn after taking the fly from the rear. It is when the fish is turning that the fly rodder has the best chance of setting the hook in the corner of the mouth.

It is worth remembering that the rules for world record fish on a fly were established by the now-defunct Saltwater Fly Rodders of America which made its headquarters at Cape May Courthouse, N.J. They were drawn up by a bunch of veteran fly rodders in 1966 and while they were all experts with the fly rod, it is doubtful any of them—with the possible exception of Stu Apte, Joe Brooks, Mark Sosin and Lee Wulff—had caught billfish on a fly at that time. The fact that they set the maximum length of the shock leader at 12 inches

Above: **The cast nets a treasure of balao.** *Facing page:* **Mate Olivio Cossio uses belly strips cut from bonito for teaser baits.**

Some veteran billfish fly rodders like to let the sailfish or marlin take the teaser bait for a few seconds to give it a taste of the fish. They claim it further excites the billfish, but I have had too many billfish swallow the teaser bait and leave after it was pulled from them. Also there is too much of a chance of the bait tearing loose and allowing the fish to swallow it. A fish that has swallowed the bait will seldom return for more.

As to the best spot to land the fly, I have found it advisable to land the fly about 6 feet to either side of the searching fish. That way the fish must turn to take the fly—giving the angler a chance to set the hook in the corner of the fish's mouth. How long a billfish hangs around the transom depends entirely on how hungry it is. While most marlin are hit-and-run predators, sailfish sometimes will stay behind the boat long enough to allow a fly rodder half a dozen casts to them. Only in cases where marlin are really hungry will they stay around long enough for more than one cast.

How long they stay around also depends on how they react to trolled lures off the outriggers or flat lines. Sometimes a sailfish—or a pod of them—will follow outrigger lures or flat line baits for several minutes before crew members see them and begin to bring the hookless lures to it. I have seen sailfish repeatedly follow and whack away at Kona head lures, plastic squids and other artificials for minutes at a time—and still come in and take a fly. Others—mostly marlin—will smash an artificial lure and leave after the first attack.

It is important for the teaser rod partner to know about billfish. A really hungry billfish can come up behind a teaser bait and engulf it before the angler realizes it. Others dawdle around behind it for what seems forever—if they are mildly hungry or curious.

Those of us who fish regularly for billfish with a fly finally settle on our own techniques for teasing up billfish and setting the hook. I used to run a hookless teaser bait out on either a flat line or an outrigger line—hoping the taste or odor of the bait would bring up billfish faster. I instructed a crew member to bring it in as rapidly as possible when fish came up so that the teaser rod man could get his bait to the fish. But I found that sailfish and marlin—mostly marlin—would smash that bait from out of nowhere and leave after swallowing it. I now use only artificial lures on the outriggers and flat lines—saving the tasty teaser bait for the last minute.

I have had a lot of time to experiment on the best

certainly indicates they knew very little about how easily a sailfish or marlin can cut a leader with a bill. The organization later turned over all its records to the I.G.F.A to administer and, unfortunately, the I.G.F.A continued to insist on the out-of-gear rule and the 12 inch shock leader length.

The first billfish fly rodders found it was better to have a partner handling the teaser rod—as crews unfamiliar with fly fishing did not always understand the technique of teasing-up billfish.

With a partner who understands how the system of teasing works, the fly rodder stands in a corner of the cockpit, fly rod in hand, while the teaser man (or woman) keeps the hookless teaser bait just ahead of the bill of the hungry billfish. When the fish is well within range of the angler—30 to 50 feet—the bait is jerked from the surface toward the boat and the fish is left wondering where its meal went. It is at that time the boat is taken out of gear, or slowed down, and the fly is cast to the billfish.

Top: **A billfish strikes at the teaser bait.** *Second down:* **A combination of a bird (and trailing school of smaller birds) and a Kona head lure works well.** *Third down:* **The author's favorite combination of lure colors to bring up billfish.** *Fourth down:* **The ideal live teaser bait—balao.**

method of attracting billfish to the surface behind the boat. During that time I have caught between 80 and 100 Pacific sailfish (and lost as many). I have found certain combinations of color and action on the part of outrigger and flat line lures seem to work best for me. Let me tell you what my system is — then you can experiment on your own. This sport is so new that nobody has all the answers.

I like to run combinations of black-and-red and yellow-and-green Kona head-type lures behind the boat. The splashing and diving action—with long bubble trails—seems to work best. Both are hookless lures. I am right-handed so I stand in the port corner of the cockpit. Because my back cast might hang up on the port outrigger line, I have the skipper stick the port rod in a rod holder up in the tower—where he can bring it in rapidly. That way the line from that rod is high enough so that it poses no obstacle to my side-ways casting.

I run the other hookless Kona head lure off the starboard outrigger, to run outside the first wake wave and perhaps 60-70 feet back—about the same distance as the port bait. I am partial to plastic squids and run them as a flat line off a cleat in the starboard corner of the cockpit. I like to run a combination of tan and pink squid back to about 30 feet behind the transom. With this rig the

teaser man can run a teaser bait on the surface about 40 feet back. He can tease the billfish quickly away from both Kona head lures or come up closer if the billfish is attracted to the squid. Either way I have a good quick shot at the searching fish. While the skipper is responsible for getting in the port Kona head, the mate brings in the starboard Kona head and—if necessary—the squid line. Usually the hookless squid are left to settle in the water.

Though most veteran billfish fly rodders—like Billy Pate—like to quickly set the hook in the corner of the mouth as the fish turns, I have adopted a new system that serves me well. I talked to a number of successful light tackle billfish anglers before I decided to try this method. They emphasized the importance of the "drop-back" in their style of fishing—with artificial lures. I figured if a billfish will begin to swallow an artificial lure on conventional light tackle, it would do the same thing with a large fly. I use double-hook 7/0 and 8/0 Mustad 34007 hooks on the flies I tie and pad them out with lots of feathers. I figure a billfish—particularly marlin—want something to eat.

First I set my drag almost on free-spool—just enough drag to prevent a backlash when the line whips off the reel. When the billfish takes the fly I don't strike when it turns but wait—the line running through the fingers of my left hand—until the fish is quite a way out and travelling away from the boat. When I figure the fish has had time to begin to swallow the big fly, then I strike. As the big, double-hooked fly pulls out of the fish's closed mouth, one or both of those sharp hooks has a very good chance of hanging up somewhere in the billfish's mouth. I have landed—and released—lots more billfish using this system than I did before.

Top: **Author watches outrigger lures.** *Right middle:* **Billy Pate keeps an eye on lures running in the boat wake.** *Right bottom:* **Pate points out leaping billfish to Capt. Bill Gannon off Quepos, Costa Rica.**

12

Venezuela's White Marlin on a Fly

Probably the best spots in the world to catch a white marlin on a fly is off the small Venezuelan port city of La Guaira in October and off Cape May, New Jersey all summer.

What makes La Guaira so interesting is that one has a very good chance of catching whites, small blue marlin and Atlantic sailfish at the same time. But the whites are small—nice fly rod size—running from about 30 pounds up to around 100 pounds, I had been planning to go there ever since I caught a 50 pound Pacific black marlin on a fly August 12, 1990 at Cape Bowling Green, Australia.

Billy Pate still holds the world record white marlin on a fly—an 80 pound fish he caught on 16 pound tippet off La Guaira September 17, 1975. The 12 pound tippet record is held by Andrew McGrath—with a 74 pound, 8 ounce fish he caught off Vitoria, Brazil on November 17,

1988. Pat Ford holds the 8 pound tippet record with a 73 pound, white he caught off La Guaira September 22, 1984.

But it wasn't weight records I was after. I just wanted to catch a white marlin on a fly.

Facing page: **Author fights stubborn Atlantic white marlin off Venezuela.** *Above:* **The acrobatic white marlin leaps far from the boat.**

In October 1990, Ed Beattie, of 5 Star Expeditions, Inc., called me up in Santa Fe to say he had been reading about my quest for all the marlin species on a fly rod and that he knew a man in Venzuela who had several sportfishing boats and would be happy to have me come down and try for a white marlin. His name was Juan Bautista Arismendi.

Since I needed a good man to handle the teaser rod and one who also spoke Spanish, I called my longtime fishing chum, the legendary San Juan River fishing guide Chuck Rizuto who lives in Farmington, N.M.

There was a gusty wind blowing across the port in the morning as we put to sea in the 38 foot Sportfisherman, *Big Lure*, skippered by Captain Hector Perez, and the seas were running a good 6-8 feet. It was a rough, pitching trip for the 1 1/2 hour run to the white marlin grounds. Johnnie, the mate, helped me put the 9 foot Sage and 8 1/2 Fisher rods together and fit them with both a Pate Marlin Reel and an Abel #5 big game reel. I had rigged both reels with 30 pound Micron backing, 100 feet of 40 pound, stretchable, Schneider mono running line and 25 feet of 12-weight, fast-sinking shooting heads.

Johnnie ran out two hookless balao baits—one on my long, 10 foot fiberglass teaser rod and the other on a 30 pound mono boat rod. He ran a couple of hookless Kona heads off the starboard outrigger—one fluorescent red and the other a bright green.

We had been trolling for about two hours when the skipper screamed "marlin!" and I stumbled to the corner of the cockpit to grab the big Fisher rod and black reel. The boat was careening in the swells and it was almost impossible to keep my footing. Chuck was already on the teaser rod and the mate was scrambling for the boat rod.

I dropped the fly into the foamy wake and looked aft. There were two dorsal fins zigzagging back and forth in the white water—alternating between the two teaser baits. Chuck had the middle teaser bait almost up to the boat and one small white marlin was right behind it.

"Alto!" I shouted to the skipper as I made a quick back cast, I could feel the boat slow as the line came forward and I saw Chuck's bait sail from the water. The marlin lunged from the water and took the fly as I gave it a quick strip.

I quickly set the hook as the marlin went off to my left and felt the hook sink in. The fish took off on a series of incredibly quick jumps—moving directly away from the boat. I raised the rod and pointed the tip at the fish as it jumped. The drag was set very lightly as I didn't want much pressure on a fish moving that quickly. There was plenty of time to increase the drag after the fish had gotten all its first jumps out of the way.

When the marlin had jumped at least a dozen times and was about 200 yards out, it sounded. I wasn't worried about it going too deep as I had nearly 900 yards of line and backing on the big black reel, but I was concerned that the white might throw the hook on one of the jumps. Billy Pate had warned me that little white marlin had tough mouths and were hard to hook.

The skipper had left the twin diesels in neutral and line was peeling off the big reel rapidly. I didn't want to get a billow of line out as that would add pressure to the 16 pound leader tippet.

That small marlin put up as tough a fight as any billfish I have ever hooked. It alternated between greyhounding jumps and deep dives, and fought all the way to the boat. It must have taken about 50 minutes to get it close enough for Johnnie to reach out and gingerly grasp the short section of 100 pound shock leader near the corner of the marlin's mouth. A second later he had the bill in his gloved hand and a sudden feeling of relief and elation washed over me as I realized the white was caught.

For anyone wanting to try for a white marlin on a fly I would suggest trying the waters off Venezuela. There are a lot of white marlin there in the fall—the best time being October and November.

Top: **An approximately 60 pound Atlantic sailfish caught on a fly by the author on the same trip.** *Bottom:* **Author and crew of** *Big Lure* **celebrate the boating of this approximately 65 pound white marlin. It was released.** *Facing page:* **A cast net is thrown over the stern to catch balao for teaser bait.**

Striped Marlin at Baja's East Cape

Both the striped marlin and a few Pacific blue marlin start arriving off the East Cape of Baja in May, but the winds tend to blow that month. The fishing picks up in June and all through the hot summer and early fall striped marlin can be found in good numbers all the way from north of La Paz down to Cabo San Lucas.

Cam Sigler and I picked June to try for both the blue and striped marlin. We fished out of that great billfish resort, Spa Buena Vista—run by an excellent angler himself, Jesus "Chuy" Valdez. Chuy insists on releasing billfish unless you want to mount—releasing billfish is an idea that appeals to me. A photo of the fish is every bit as good as a mount and the fish is allowed to grow larger for another angler.

Spa Buena Vista is close to Punta Arena—a point of land that juts out into the Sea of Cortez from the east coast of Baja. It is a famous area for roosterfish—which feed right along the surf line. I have caught a number of them on a fly—fishing from an outboard motor-powered panga—and it is an exciting sport.

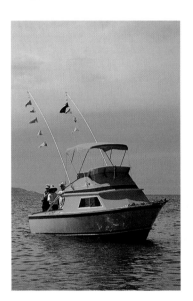

Chuy assigned Cam and me to the 38 foot *Rafialita* captained by Jose Ramon Montano. The mate was jovial Barulio Ortiz, who didn't seem to have much confidence in the long fly rods we handed him from the panga. Chuy has a few crews trained to fish fly rodders, but this was not one of them. It didn't matter as I was used to introducing new crews to fly fishing. Most of the Mexican crews on the East Cape were skeptical about fly rods a few years ago, but a lot of them are now enthusiastic about the flies and long rods after seeing a lot of billfish caught on them. The reluctance to accept fly rods is understandable when one considers the history of these Baja fishermen. Most of them are second or third generation deep sea fishermen. It is their nature to fish with

---

Above: **The entire fleet of Chuy Valdez's sportfishing boats are colored bright yellow.** *Facing page:* **Pacific striped marlin takes to the air off the East Cape of Baja as author raises rod tip—and prays.**

large hooks and heavy tackle—big rods, 50-80 pound mono and either trolled dead bait or live bait. When fish strike, the skipper jams the throttle forward so that the angler can more easily set the hook.

Along come we fly rodders and ask them to (1) troll baits without any hooks in them and (2) stop the boat when a billfish comes up to the trolled bait. No wonder they think we are a little crazy. But once they see how fly fishing works, they become enthusiastic. It is worth remembering one thing, however, many of the crews (at spots like Cabo San Lucas) make money by selling billfish at the dock. Find this out before going fishing with them — and if you want to release your fish—offer to pay them something extra (like $50) to release fish. Most will agree to it as a sure $50 is better than nothing—there are days when no fish are caught.

The day was calm as the *Rafialita* nosed gently into the smooth swells of the Sea of Cortez. Schools of porpoise moved off toward the horizon and frigate birds circled high above, searching for schools of baitfish. Cam and I rigged my favorite system of outrigger Kona heads and flat lines.

"Marleen," the skipper said softly, pointing off to our port side. A striped marlin was lazily swimming on the calm surface—not more then 100 yards away. He swung the boat toward the fish and we towed the teasers past him

twice, but the fish was not hungry. It submerged a few minutes later and we continued trolling in an easterly direction.

It grew hot as the sun rose in the eastern sky and no breeze blew. A dorado slashed in from nowhere and smashed one of the Kona heads—only to leave when it found no tasty meat to swallow.

A big blue marlin suddenly surfaced between the Kona heads and the mullet teaser disappeared in a burst of white water before Cam could get to the teaser rod and before I could grab the fly rod from the port corner of the cockpit.

'Whew!" was all Cam could say as we both stared at the spot where the big blue had struck—and gone.

"Marlin azul," Jose said, shaking his head. "Need big boat rod and big hooks."

I smiled at Cam. "Someday." I said.

The two striped marlin came up an hour later as we were both sprawled in fighting chairs—staring at the brassy sea. The first thing I heard was the loud thud as the mate, Barulio, hit the deck of the cockpit from where he had been watching the baits above.

"Marleen!" he shouted, grabbing for the flat line of plastic squid. As I rose I could see the dorsal fin of a marlin just behind the last squid. Another black dorsal fin was zigzagging just behind the port Kona head.

"I got the teaser," Cam yelled grabbing the rod. I picked

A big striped marlin begins to tire and author leads it close to boat—wearing fighting harness and belt socket for long fights.

up the fly rod from the corner of the cockpit and dropped the fly over the transom—letting it run back about 20 feet on the surface.

"Alto!" I shouted to Jose—asking him to slow to a stop. He was too intent on the billfish to hear.

"Two striped marleen!" he shouted back—waving at the wake behind the boat. Too busy to care whether the boat was in gear or not, I made a back cast and dropped the big, double-hooked green mackerel fly as close to the skidding mullet as I could. The fly immediately disappeared as a marlin rolled over on it.

I pointed the rod tip at the fish and let it take line through the fingers of my left hand. I stepped back—letting the coils of line on the deck whip out through the rod guides. I struck twice when the line was cleared—clamping the line between my left palm and the rod. The marlin felt the hook and went straight up into the air.

"Aieee!" screamed Barulio as the fish twisted in the sunlight.

The striped marlin began a series of greyhounding jumps that took it out to the horizon in a matter of seconds. Of all the marlin, I think the striped is the most acrobatic—and the most fun to catch on a fly rod.

The marlin made 12 jumps before sounding. I strapped on a belt socket and played the fish as it stubbornly stayed down for about 15 minutes. Jose—an old hand at this game—slowly moved the boat forward and planed the fish upward until it began to jump again. After a series of a half dozen jumps the striped marlin dove and went down and down, and down. The spool of the big golden fly reel kept revolving until, at last, the fish stopped, way below.

Sweat ran down my face and soaked my shirt as the big 15-weight Fisher rod bent. The three man watched intently as I played the big billfish in the silence. Only the mutter of the big diesel engine broke the stillness.

"Watch the rod," Jose warned.

After nearly 40 minutes the fish began to come up. I pumped as Barulio got a small bill gaff ready and Jose slipped on a pair of cloth gloves. As the fish came alongside, Barulio slipped the gaff over the bill and led it close. Jose grasped the bill and the two men slid the wet marlin over the side.

Cam grinned and we shook hands silently. The crew slid the striped marlin—which we estimated at about 100-125 pounds—onto the transom for photos. After taking the photos, Cam removed the fly from the mouth and the marlin was slid over the side. I waved good-bye as the tired fish swam away on the surface.

"Good," Jose grinned. "Fly rod works pretty good," he said as Barulio nodded.

I grinned back. It was enough. There were two more Mexican crewmen who saw the fun and sport of fly fishing for billfish.

Author shows big dorsal fin of striped marlin—at least as high as body width. Pacific blue marlin dorsal is about half as big—the best way to tell them apart. Marlin was released.

14

Reels
For Billfish

While all the fly tackle used to catch sailfish and marlin is important, the single most important item is the fly reel. Without a sophisticated drag system and a large line and backing capacity a reel is useless in trying to stop these fast and powerful game fish.

You get what you pay for in this sport. I have seen fly rodders try to cut corners on reels and have watched them lose fish they might have landed on a good reel. It takes a well-machined piece of equipment to handle a sailfish or marlin greyhounding across the surface of the sea at somewhere around 60 mph.

A problem for a big saltwater billfish reel is saltwater. These highly-engineered reels must first be anodized against saltwater corrosion and that means throughout. Every screw and spring must be saltwater resistant or it will fail under stress.

Earlier saltwater reels were made of cast aluminum. The process proved unsatisfactory and today's big game reels are machined from solid blocks of aircraft-quality aluminum and stainless steel bar stock. The drag systems utilize stainless steel bearings, multiple-disc surfaces of metal, Teflon and cork and the spools are also machined from the same quality 6061-T6 aircraft aluminum. These fast-spinning spools are counterbalanced to within a few grains of weight.

Facing page: **Three of the most popular marlin fly reels on the market (left to right) Abel No. 5 reel, the Fin-Nor No. 5 reel and the Billy Pate Marlin Reel.** *Above:* **Three excellent sailfish reels (left to right) Abel No. 4 reel, the STH Grand Slam reel and Scientific Angler/3M System Two Model 1213 reel.**

As a result, these big game fly reels do not come cheap. The best sell from $500 to $1,500 and some specially-made Titanium reels sell for thousands of dollars.

A big game reel that will handle sailfish should have a spool capacity of about 350-400 yards of 30 pound Micron or braided Dacron backing and a 30 foot shooting head. Obviously these reels will easily handle Atlantic sailfish—which today average about 40 pounds off the East Coast of the U.S. However, they must also be able to handle the bigger Pacific sailfish—which can easily average 100 pounds.

Capacities on these reels have been greatly increased by the development of the new Spectra and Kevlar lines— with much-decreased diameters. Some of the lines—with virtually no stretch—can increase these reel capacities up to 800-1,000 yards. Lines like the Fenwick Iron Thread, Ripcord line from Cabella—braided from 100 percent Spectra (a gel-spun polyethylene fiber)—have re-defined reel capacity. These lines—with the line test equal to the Micron and Dacron, but with sizes 1/3 to 1/2 the diameter—have revolutionized freshwater fishing.

But I add one word of caution in using these new lines as backing for big game fly fishing. These lines are so hard it is difficult to cut them with a pair of nail clippers. If these lines are used for big game fly reel backing be very careful not to grasp these lines while they are ripping off a reel! Because of the hardness of the line they can easily sever a finger or deliver a severe cut to the palm of your hand. If you use them be sure to keep the billfish "on the reel" while fighting it.

Some good sailfish reels are the Billy Pate Tarpon Reel, the Abel #4, the Fin-Nor 945 AR, the Orvis DXR 4" diameter tarpon reel, the STH Grand Slam, the Charlton 8500 Signature series (completely sealed) reel, the Ari Hart ATH S3, the Scientific Angler (3M) Model 11 1213 and the Model 111. The venerable Seamaster is still being used for big game but the company has come out with some excellent new models. The Seamaster 111—with 300 yards

of 30 pound backing and a fly line, could be considered a sailfish reel.

I include the Scientific Angler's Model 1213 and the Martin 12D reels even though they do not fall into the same category as the other reels—quality-wise or price-wise. However both have about a 400-yard backing capacity and fair drag systems. They are adequate reels for the big game fly fisherman on a budget—both sell in the neighborhood of $150.

However when it comes to fly reels for marlin, there are not many that qualify. Remember that marlin can run anywhere from 100-400 pounds for fly fishermen and a 400 pound Pacific blue marlin is a far cry from a sailfish! They travel at tremendous speeds and dive to incredible depths. It takes a special kind of saltwater fly reel to handle such fish. I consider a marlin reel one that has a space-age drag system and a capacity of at least 600 yards of 30 pound backing. There are a few reels that are borderline cases—such as the Abel 4.5 reel with a capacity of 450 yards of 30 pound backing and a shooting head. The fact that this reel has the side plates beefed-up to withstand considerably more expansion pressure than most fly reels and can accommodate 30 pound mono as backing, may qualify it as a marlin reel. The high stretch factor of mono can compensate for a loss of backing capacity.

I classify the Billy Pate Marlin Reel, the Abel #5, the Fin-Nor 925-AR (#5) and the Seamaster Marlin One and Marlin Two as the best. The Pate has a capacity of 600+ yards of 30 pound backing— plus a 30 foot shooting head, the Fin-Nor a 750 yard capacity, the Abel 5 a 900 yard capacity, the Seamaster Marlin One 700 yards and the Marlin Two 1,000 yards of 30 pound backing.

Whether a big game reel is direct-drive or anti-reverse depends entirely on the preference of the angler. I know big game fly fishermen who swear by the direct-drive and claim it gives them more control over the fish. I happen to like anti-reverse reels because they are more forgiving of mistakes on the part of the fly rodder and I make a lot of mistakes.

I wind with my left hand because I have found I can exert more pressure on a big fish with my stronger right arm, but—again—it depends upon the angler. However you wind, be sure to tell the manufacturer which hand you wind with when ordering a reel. Some of the more sophisticated reels need to be modified at the factory.

Above top: **The new Charlton 8600 (sealed) fly reel is excellent for sailfish—with a highly-machined drag system.** *Bottom:* **The Abel No. 5 reel has capacity of 900 yards of 30 pound backing.** *Facing page:* **Perhaps the finest all-around reel for *big billfish* on the market is the Billy Pate Marlin Reel—with an anti-reverse drag system.**

The Elusive Pacific Blue Marlin

Nine years from the day I caught the little 43 pound Atlantic blue marlin on a fly off Jamaica—and began my quest for the rest of them—I started 1992 off badly.

I knew there was really no one place where the Pacific blue could be found in any numbers—at least not in sizes suitable for a fly rodder.

The Atlantic blue can be found in fair numbers off St. Thomas in the Virgin Islands, in the Cayman Islands, Jamaica, off Venezuela, off the East Coast of the U.S. in the summer months, off Walker Cay, Bimini, Cat Cay and the Berry Islands in the Bahamas, and between the island of Cozumel and the east coast of Mexico from March through May each year.

But the Pacific blue marlin, which is migratory, is difficult to locate in numbers small enough to take on a fly rod—100-400 pounds. They can be found anywhere in the great Pacific Ocean. They are frequent off Hawaii, but are usually big fish—far too big for a fly fisherman. As a matter of fact they are too big for a fly fisherman almost everywhere.

I had hooked and lost a few off Panama, Costa Rica and Baja California. I never had one on for more than a few minutes. The blue marlin is a very different kind of fish from the others of his tribe. It is the undisputed king of the marlin family. The white, the black and the striped marlin will often come up behind a teaser bait and tentatively whack away at it with a bill. They occasionally follow the baits for a while before making up their minds to either leave or strike.

But the blue marlin seldom gives any warning before it strikes. It is pure predator—travelling at a high rate of

Los Padres—the huge rocks at the tip of the Baja Penninsula—just outside Cabo San Lucas, Mexico.

speed and with a vicious strike. Ever notice how many boats are named the *Blue Marlin*, or the *Marlin Azul* in Spanish-speaking countries?

I had a smashing strike on an outrigger bait in January 1992 by a streaking blue marlin off Mazatlan. Luis, the skipper of the Star Fleet boat *Vega*, laughed and grinned at his son and mate, Ramon—shaking his head ruefully.

"Marlin azul," he said simply.

In February I fished out of that great billfish resort in Panama—Tropic Star Lodge. I fished alone—as usual—and the seas were rough and the wind brutal. My fishing pals, Skipper Isuaro Urrutia and mate Olivio Cossio, knew the chances were remote we would take a blue on a fly, but they gave it their best.

At about 2 p.m. a billfish crashed a teaser lure and took my fly in a white geyser of foam. It made two towering jumps off to my right and I lost it from sight as Isuaro swung the boat to port to follow the leaping fish. I had that

blue on for about 20 minutes before he broke me off. Both men told me the fish was in the neighborhod of 400 pounds and both agreed I had bitten off more than I could chew on a fly rod!

Billy Pate was also trying to catch a Pacific blue marlin that spring and finally hooked about a 400 pound blue while fishing off Quepos, Costa Rica in March. He fought that fish—standing up without a belt socket—for 7 1/2 hours as the boat drifted out to sea. When it finally began to grow dark the crew insisted they cut the marlin off. There is a hard and fast rule about coming in at dark in that part of the world. It was especially tragic for Pate because he had the marlin up to within 25 feet of the boat twice, but they couldn't reach it with a gaff.

By that summer my wife, Victoria, was hinting darkly that the monthly failures to catch a blue were starting to take on the aspects of a Holy Grail. The only one who

thought my dedication normal was Billy Pate.

So it was with a sense of deja vu that I accepted my friend Eric Heimpel's kind invitation to fish for four days aboard one of his Star Fleet boats, the *Elinor*, out of Cabo San Lucas in August.

"The blues are here," Eric said on the phone. "Not many, but a few and small ones at that. Our boats are averaging a couple of stripes a day and a blue every other day or so."

That was about as good an average as anyone in the world is ever going to get for Pacific blue marlin on a fly—anywhere. Cam Sigler, my big game fishing chum from Vashon Island, Washington, called me the night before I left.

"I'm no mathematician," he said, "but you got any idea what the odds are of you catching that blue when you already have six billfish species on a fly and need the seventh?"

I tried not to think about it.

It was warm and still at the dock in Cabo San Lucas that morning of August 17th. The sun was just below the horizon, and thin bands of clouds hung just above the eastern sea surface—a skein of black lace.

Captain Martin Gonzales grinned as I handed him the two fly rods and climbed aboard.

"One more time," he said. "Maybe this time. Quien sabe—who knows?"

I shook hands with Guillermo Estrada, the mate, and roughed up the tousled hair of 14-year-old Ivan Gomez, the youngest member of the crew.

"Where's Jerry?" I asked, stowing two bags just inside the big cabin. Jerry Cevallos, manager of the Star Fleet, had said the night before he wanted to come along to see what fly fishing was all about.

"Getting coffee," Martin said, pointing down the dock before climbing into the tower. I looked up to see the stocky frame of Jerry coming down the dock with a paper tray of steaming coffee cups.

The jagged outline of Los Padres—the huge, rugged rocks jutting up from the quiet sea—loomed off our starboard bow as the old 43 foot wooden hull of the *Elinor* nosed into the first of the big Pacific swells just outside the harbor.

"We try Gordo Banks, O.K?" Martin shouted from the tower. I nodded back. The banks, 8-10 miles up the coast off Punta Gorda and just east of San Jose del Cabo, could be productive when other areas were not.

The ride took nearly two hours, and I watched the arid, rugged coast from the fighting chair. Guillermo and I rigged the hookless outrigger Kona heads and got them ready. Martin had obtained a large, foot-long "Macho Lisa" mullet from a local fisherman. It would ride between the two outrigger baits on a flat line.

The sun was more than an hour up and it was already hot when Martin throttled back and we put the lures and

baits out. I ran a daisy chain of tan-colored plastic squid about 20 feet back from the starboard corner of the transom. I had one of my own 7/0 double-hooked multi-colored flies rigged on the end of the 100 pound length of shock leader. It was tied to resemble a small dorado, or dolphinfish. Ahead of it I had slid a soft, white foam popper festooned with pink tail feathers. The fly was extremely colorful and I laid it on top of the transom in the port corner of the cockpit while I stripped off line and fed it into an empty plastic bucket at my feet.

I was using a medium, 15-weight Fisher Blue Water fly rod and a No. 5 Fin-Nor anti-reverse reel with about 600 yards of 36 pound Green Spot backing. The 30 foot shooting head was a Cortland prototype 15-S fast-sinking line with a beefed-up core of 518 grains and a breaking strength of between 45 and 50 pounds. The class tippet was 20 pound Mason mono.

The green-and-yellow Kona head on the port outrigger and the red-and-black one on the starboard 'rigger were diving and churning in the moderate chop as I ran the fly back about 20 feet to see how it looked in the water. The big, hookless mullet splashed on the surface between the two outrigger lures.

I glanced at my wristwatch. It was 8:45 a.m. I started to bring the fly in when I saw a flash beneath the port lure. Suddenly there was an explosion of white water and the lure disappeared.

"Marlin!" Martin screamed from the tower and I made one back cast—turning to see that my fly missed the port outrigger line. I cast the fly in the general direction of the port 'rigger lure—trying to land the big fly close to where I had seen the strike. The marlin took the fly in a vicious strike as soon as it hit the water.

Martin had no time to take the boat out of gear—automatically disqualifying the marlin as a world record fish by International Game Fish Association rules. I couldn't have cared less. I was frantically holding on to the bowed rod as

the marlin began a series of greyhounding leaps off to our left. I struck hard twice as I saw the big glistening shape climb into the sunlit sky—then looked down to see if the line was cleared.

"Ai-yai-yai!" screamed Jerry off to my left as Martin spun the wheel to starboard to follow the leaping marlin.

"Eight, nine, ten, eleven..." he shouted down from the bridge, counting jumps. I looked down at the backing melting rapidly from the big golden reel.

"Fifteen, sixteen, seventeen jumps!" Martin shrieked from the tower.

And suddenly the line went slack. I felt a sickening sensation in the pit of my stomach. There was only a bit of backing left on the reel. I *knew* the blue had broken off. Martin was backing down as rapidly as the old, single diesel would go. Suddenly there was tension on the line again.

"Reel, reel!" Martin shouted as I tried to quickly gain line—hoping against hope that the marlin would remain hooked. Jerry slipped a rod belt around my waist and I jammed the rod butt into the leather socket and settled down for what I knew was going to be a long battle.

The fight lasted no longer than an hour—miraculously. I fully expected to be there all day with that fish, but the marlin came in steadily as we backed down. When it came close to the boat I *knew* it was going to start jumping again. It didn't. When I finally had it alongside, Guillermo reached out with the longhandled gaff and led the tired marlin to the boat by the bill. Ivan hung over the side and grasped the bill. Martin slipped the boat control into neutral and leaped down to the deck—where he quickly slipped a rope around the tail of the marlin.

When the three crewmen—helped by Jerry and me—slid the marlin over the gunwale, pandemonium broke loose. There were "high-fives," backslaps, handshakes, war dances and embraces all over the cockpit. It was the first Pacific blue marlin caught on a fly at Cabo and I had my Grand Slam.

There was never a more beautiful day off the Cape of Baja California. The leading hook of the fly had sunk into the corner of the marlin's mouth and the trailing 7/0 stainless steel hook had buried itself in the roof of the big fish's mouth—probably the reason the fish had fought no harder.

I reached out and softly patted the wet side of the inert marlin—a gift fish.

It was the only marlin I ever kept. Eric Heimpel wanted it mounted on the wall of the Star Fleet headquarters.

It was weighed later on-shore by Luis Bulnes, my friend, and I.G.F.A representative for Cabo San Lucas. It weighed 176 pounds.

Above: **After nine years of trying for the Grand Slam of billfishing on a fly—a picture is worth a thousand words!** *Facing page top:* **Everybody on board—including the author—lends a hand to bring the big Pacific blue marlin over the gunwale!** *Bottom:* **The front 7/0 stainless steel hook was set in the corner of the marlin's mouth while the rear hook was sunk in the roof of the fish's mouth—probably why it fought no longer than an hour.**

16

Catch-and-Release
Versus Records

In this day of commercial longlining, deep sea netting and environmental concern for our dwindling

resources, we fly rodders who fish the ocean for big game fish should be leaders in the catch-and-release field.

Years ago we kept our billfish—whether to have them mounted as trophies or to show them off to our

friends at the dock. It was a macho thing to do and I wish now we had released all those fish we caught on reg-

ular big game tackle. But since going after billfish with a fly rod, most of us have let our fish go. It has become

a trademark of the fly fisherman. However there are still far too many billfish—caught on a fly—that end up

hanging from scales on the dock.

Thanks to Herculean efforts by such organizations as the prestigious Billfish Foundation, the Sportfishing

Council of Game Conservation International and the Fisheries Defense Fund, Inc., most big game tourna-

ments today have become catch-and-release events. The I.G.F.A.—in spite of its emphasis on recordkeeping—

has pushed for release tournaments also.

No one wants to stamp out fly fishing for record fish—just keep

down the instances where fly-caught billfish are injured or killed.

Any fly rodder who thinks he or she has a billfish that might qual-

ify for a world record should be absolutely sure of the record

weights before bringing the fish in to be measured and weighed.

We have a very good system today of estimating the weight of

billfish. The girth of the fish should be measured with a tape mea-

sure and then squared.

Facing page: **Author waves goodbye to an approximately 100 pound striped marlin—after releasing it off Baja's East Cape.**
Above: **A big sailfish just before being released off Costa Rica.**

That figure is then multiplied by the length (from the tip of the lower jaw to the fork in the tail) and that number is then divided by 800. The result should be within 10 pounds of the actual weight of the fish. This can be done as soon as the fish is boated and if there is any doubt about the fish being a record, it should be released.

As anyone who has tried it knows, the meat of marlin and sailfish is anything but tasty. It is strong and very greasy—making very poor eating. The fact that many people in Mexico and Central America eat billfish doesn't mean it is a gourmet's delight. They need the protein.

I got a cool reception from a number of record fishermen and a few tournament publications when I advocated fishing for fun and not worrying about all the I.G.F.A. rules and regulations. These people have scared some beginners into thinking they have broken some law by trolling flies, casting while a boat is still in gear, using shock leaders longer than the 12 inches required by I.G.F.A for world records and using leaders stronger than the I.G.F.A classes of 2, 4, 6, 8, 12, 16 and 20 pound-test.

Lighten up, Gents. Fly fishing for billfish is supposed to be fun! The only rules are those established long ago by the Saltwater Fly Rodders of America and later by the I.G.F.A—both record-keeping organizations, not regulatory agencies. The only thing illegal a fly fisherman can do while billfishing is something that breaks a local, state or federal law.

Most of us try to make sure the boat is either in neutral, or slowed down, when we cast a fly at billfish—not because we have to but because it is far easier to hook a billfish with a fly at slow speeds. We want the sail or marlin to take the fly as it turns so the hook can be set in the corner of the mouth. It is very difficult—if not impossible—to set a hook in the tough, thorny bill of a billfish which is whacking away at a fly at high speeds.

For the vast majority of us who fly fish for billfish and release most of our fish, there are no rules of any kind, other than sportsmanship—self-imposed rules that keep us from maiming, gaffing or otherwise injuring fish we are going to release.

Many of the great pioneer saltwater fly fishermen did not fish for records. Webster "Doc" Robinson—who caught the first sailfish and marlin on a fly—seldom entered any of his billfish for reords. Winston Moore, a marvelous saltwater fly rodder—who has caught more than 100 Pacific sailfish on a fly—never submitted a billfish for a record. Neither did that West Coast saltwater fly rod legend, Harry Kime.

There is a small contingent of fly rodders—like my friend, the legendary Billy Pate—and a handful of others like Stu Apte, Bob Stearns, Pat Ford, Jim Gray, Ray Beadle, Charlie Owen, and Ed Rice—who regularly fish for world records. For these guys—and a few others—the I.G.F.A rules are very important. They should adhere to them strictly. But by over-emphasizing the I.G.F.A world record rules for all fly fishing for billfish, some are misleading a lot of newcomers into believing they are doing something wrong or illegal by not following I.G.F.A record rules when fishing for fun.

The vast majority of us who fish for billfish on a fly do it for the thrill of the sport and to release our fish. In order to obtain a world record one needs to kill the billfish to weigh and measure it. Of the hundreds of billfish I have caught on a fly, not one has been submitted for a world record. And—as fellow anglers who were with me can testify—a number of the last marlin I caught, if submitted, would have been world records on 20 pound class tippet.

I fished with—and clearly remember—the late, great Lee Wulff, whose creed was: "A good game fish is too valuable to be caught only once. The fish you release is your gift to another angler."

Letting the water run through a black marlin's gills before releasing it off the Australian coast.

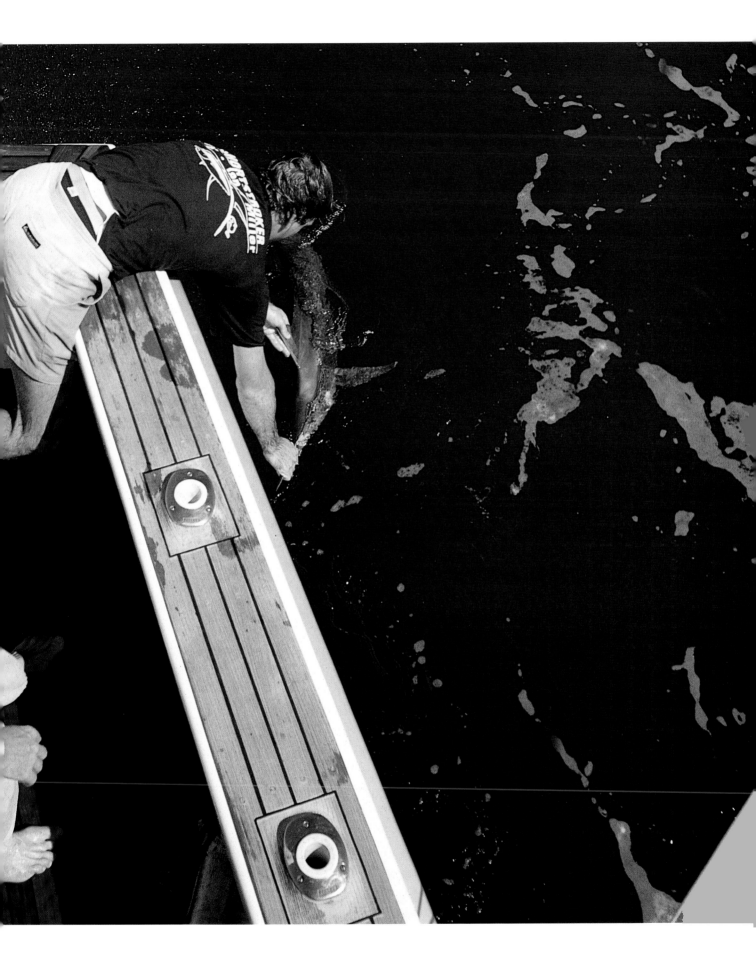

Also By Jack Samson

Trap And Skeet Shooting *1971*

Line Down! The Special
World of Big Game Fishing *1973*

The Best of Corey Ford *(Edited) 1974*

The Sportsman's World *1976*

The Worlds of Ernest Thompson Seton *1976*

Falconry Today *1976*

A Fine and Pleasant Misery *(Edited) 1978*

Successful Outdoor Writing *1979*

The Bear Book *(Edited) 1979*

The Pond *1979*

The Grizzly Book *(Edited) 1978*

The Great Fish *1983*

Modern Falconry *1984*

Hunting the Southwest *1985*

Chennault—A Biography *1988*

Cetreria *1987*

Salt Water Fly Fishing *1991*

Wind Knots and Near Misses *1995*

Lee Wulff *1995*